ECOLOGY AND EVOLUTION

SCIENCE EDUCATION FOR PUBLIC UNDERSTANDING PROGRAM

UNIVERSITY OF CALIFORNIA AT BERKELEY
LAWRENCE HALL OF SCIENCE LHS

RONKONKOMA, NEW YORK

This book is part of SEPUP's middle school science course sequence:

Science and Life Issues

- My Body and Me
- Micro-Life
- Our Genes, Our Selves
- Ecology and Evolution
- Using Tools and Ideas

Issues, Evidence and You

- Water Usage and Safety
- Materials Science
- Energy
- Environmental Impact

Additional SEPUP instructional materials include:

CHEM-2 (Chemicals, Health, Environment and Me): Grades 4–6

SEPUP Modules: Grades 7–12

Science and Sustainability: Course for Grades 10–12

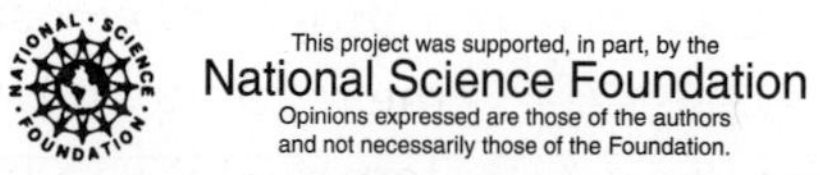

1 2 3 4 5 6 7 8 9 06 05 04 03 02 01

ISBN: 1-887725-39-3

SEPUP
Lawrence Hall of Science
University of California at Berkeley
Berkeley CA 94720-5200

e-mail: sepup@uclink4.berkeley.edu
Website: www.sepuplhs.org

Published by:

17 Colt Court
Ronkonkoma NY 11779
Website: www.lab-aids.com

A Letter to SALI Students

As you examine the activities in this book, you may wonder, "Why does this book look so different from other science books I've seen?" The reason is simple: it is a different kind of science program, and only some of what you will learn can be seen by leafing through this book!

Science and Life Issues, or *SALI,* uses several kinds of activities to teach science. For example, you will design and conduct an experiment to investigate human responses. You will explore a model of how species compete for food. And you will play the roles of scientists learning about the causes of infectious disease. A combination of experiments, readings, models, debates, role plays, and projects will help you uncover the nature of science and the relevance of science to your interests.

You will find that important scientific ideas come up again and again in different activities. You will be expected to do more than just memorize these concepts: you will be asked to explain and apply them. In particular, you will improve your decision-making skills, using evidence and weighing outcomes to decide what you think should be done about scientific issues facing society.

How do we know that this is a good way for you to learn? In general, research on science education supports it. In particular, the activities in this book were tested by hundreds of students and their teachers, and they were modified on the basis of their feedback. In a sense, this entire book is the result of an investigation: we had people test our ideas, we interpreted the results, and we revised our ideas! We believe the result will show you that learning more about science is important, enjoyable, and relevant to your life.

SALI Staff

SEPUP STAFF

Dr. Herbert D. Thier, Program Director
Dr. Barbara Nagle, Co-Director
Laura Baumgartner, Instructional Materials Developer
Asher Davison, Instructional Materials Developer
Manisha Hariani, Instructional Materials Developer
Daniel Seaver, Instructional Materials Developer
Dr. Marcelle Siegel, Instructional Materials Developer
Marlene Thier, Teacher Education and CHEM Coordinator
Dr. Peter J. Kelly, Research Associate (England)
Dr. Magda Medir, Research Associate (Spain)
Mike Reeske, Development Associate
Miriam Shein, Publications Coordinator
Sylvia Parisotto, Publications Assistant
Roberta Smith, Administrative Coordinator
Judy Greenspan, Administrative Assistant
Donna Anderson, Administrative Assistant

CONTRIBUTORS/DEVELOPERS

Barbara Nagle
Manisha Hariani
Herbert D. Thier
Asher Davison
Susan K. Boudreau
Daniel Seaver
Laura Baumgartner

TEACHER CONTRIBUTORS

Kathaleen Burke
Richard Duquin
Donna Markey

CONTENT AND SCIENTIFIC REVIEW

Peter J. Kelly, Emeritus Professor of Education and Senior Visiting Fellow, School of Education, University of Southampton, Southampton, England

Eric Meikle, National Center for Science Education, Oakland, California

Deborah Penry, Assistant Professor, Department of Integrative Biology, University of California at Berkeley, Berkeley, California

RESEARCH ASSISTANCE

Marcelle Siegel, Leif Asper

PRODUCTION

Project coordination: Miriam Shein
Production and composition: Seventeenth Street Studios
Cover concept: Maryann Ohki
Photo research and permissions: Sylvia Parisotto
Editing: WordWise

Field Test Centers

The classroom is SEPUP's laboratory for development. We are extremely appreciative of the following center directors and teachers who taught the program during the 1998–99 and 1999–2000 school years. These teachers and their students contributed significantly to improving the course.

REGIONAL CENTER, SOUTHERN CALIFORNIA

Donna Markey, *Center Director*
Kim Blumeyer, Helen Copeland, Pat McLoughlin, Donna Markey, Philip Poniktera, Samantha Swann, Miles Vandegrift

REGIONAL CENTER, IOWA

Dr. Robert Yager and Jeanne Bancroft, *Center Directors*
Rebecca Andresen, Lore Baur, Dan Dvorak, Dan Hill, Mark Kluber, Amy Lauer, Lisa Martin, Stephanie Phillips

REGIONAL CENTER, WESTERN NEW YORK

Dr. Robert Horvat, *Center Director*
Kathaleen Burke, Mary Casion, Dick Duquin, Eleanor Falsone, Lillian Gondree, Jason Mayle, James Morgan, Valerie Tundo

JEFFERSON COUNTY, KENTUCKY

Pamela Boykin, *Center Director*
Charlotte Brown, Tara Endris, Sharon Kremer, Karen Niemann, Susan Stinebruner, Joan Thieman

LIVERMORE, CALIFORNIA

Scott Vernoy, *Center Director*
Rick Boster, Ann Ewing, Kathy Gabel, Sharon Schmidt, Denia Segrest, Bruce Wolfe

QUEENS, NEW YORK

Pam Wasserman, *Center Director*
Gina Clemente, Cheryl Dodes, Karen Horowitz, Tricia Hutter, Jean Rogers, Mark Schmucker, Christine Wilk

TUCSON, ARIZONA

Jonathan Becker, *Center Director*
Peggy Herron, Debbie Hobbs, Carol Newhouse, Nancy Webster

INDEPENDENT

Berkeley, California: Robyn McArdle
Fresno, California: Al Brofman
Orinda, California: Sue Boudreau, Janine Orr, Karen Snelson
Tucson, Arizona: Patricia Cadigan, Kevin Finegan

Contents

UNIT E Ecology

UNIT F Evolution

Ecology

E

Unit E

Ecology

Michael loved to bike through the park. The air smelled fresher there than on the street, and he always saw so many interesting things.

Once, he had come across a bird's nest with several young chicks still in it. As he watched, one of the parents had brought food for the chicks to eat. He wondered if he would see anything like that today.

Suddenly, he saw a small frog near the edge of Turtle Pond. It looked very familiar. In fact, it looked just like the frog his sister kept as a pet. It was different from the frogs he usually saw at Turtle Pond.

"Could that be my sister's frog?" Michael wondered. If so, how did it get there? Did it escape, or could his sister have let it go? Could a pet frog survive in Turtle Pond? How would it affect the other animals that also lived in the pond?

• • •

What are the relationships between an organism and its environment? What effect do humans have on these relationships?

In this unit, you will explore ecology: the study of the relationships between organisms, including humans, and the environment.

72 The Miracle Fish?

Have you ever thought that it would be cool to have parrots flying around in your backyard? Or wished that there were hippos in your local lake? What happens when you introduce an organism into a new environment?

FISHING ON LAKE VICTORIA

James Abila is a Kenyan boy of 17. His family has a small fishing boat on Lake Victoria. He sat outside his hut to talk to us. Inside, his mother was preparing lunch, while his sister and younger brother were laying out a few fish to dry in the afternoon sun.

Uganda
Kenya
Lake Victoria
Tanzania

James started his story. "My father made our boat. He was always one of the best fishermen in the village. He still catches all kinds of fish, though he says it's not as easy as it used to be. Most of the fish in the lake used to be very small, just 2–4 inches long. So it was easy to use our net to catch hundreds of small fish. But about the time I was born, the number of fish seemed to go down. Luckily, the government introduced new fish into the lake. Now, the most common fish in the lake is Nile perch. It's a much bigger fish and can be too heavy to catch with a net. That's why I work for one of the fishing companies. They have the large boats needed to catch Nile perch. And I can earn money to help feed my family."

CHALLENGE

What are the trade-offs of introducing a species into a new environment?

PROCEDURE

Work with your group to read and discuss the story of Nile perch in Lake Victoria.

NILE PERCH

Lake Victoria is the second largest lake in the world and it contains some extremely large fish. One type of fish found there, known as Nile perch *(Lates niloticus),* can grow to 240 kilograms (530 pounds), though its average size is 3–6 kilograms (7–13 pounds). But Nile perch weren't always found in Lake Victoria. Until the 1980s, the most common fish in Lake Victoria were cichlids (SICK-lids), small freshwater fish about 2–4 inches long. (If you've ever seen aquarium fish such as oscars, Jack Dempseys, or freshwater angelfish, you've seen a cichlid.)

This man is holding a large Nile perch.

Lake Victoria cichlids interest **ecologists**—scientists who study relationships between organisms and environments—because there are so many species of these fish. Although they all belong to the same family (see Figure 1), at one time there were over 300 different species of cichlids in Lake Victoria. Almost 99% of these species could not be found anywhere else in the world!

Figure 1: Classification of Cichlids	
Kingdom	Animalia
Phylum	Chordata
Class	Osteichthyes (bony fish)
Family	Cichlidae

There used to be many other kinds of fish in the lake, including catfish, carp, and lungfish. The 30 million people who lived around Lake Victoria relied on the lake for food. Because most of the fish were small, they could be caught by using simple fishing nets and a canoe. The fish were then dried in the sun and sold locally.

By the late 1950s, however, it appeared the lake was being overfished. So many fish were caught that the populations remaining did not have enough members left to reproduce and grow. If the lake continued to be overfished, there might not be enough fish left for people to eat. As a result, the British government (which ruled this part of Africa

Cichlids are one of the many small fish commonly found in Lake Victoria.

at that time) decided to introduce new fish species, such as Nile perch, into the lake. They wanted to increase the amount of fish that was available to eat; they hoped to provide more high-protein fish for local people and to be able to sell extra fish to other countries. Ecologists were opposed to this idea. They were worried that the introduction of Nile perch, which had no natural enemies within the lake, would negatively affect the lake's ecosystem. Before a final decision could be made, Nile perch were secretly added into the lake. Eventually, more Nile perch were deliberately added by the government in the early 1960s.

During the 1960s and 1970s, before there were a lot of Nile perch in the lake, about 100,000 metric tons of fish (including cichlids) were caught each year. By 1989, the total catch of fish from Lake Victoria had increased to 500,000 metric tons. Today, each of the three countries surrounding the lake (Uganda, Kenya, and Tanzania) sells extra fish to other countries. In Figure 2, you can see how the amount of fish caught by Kenyan fisheries has changed over a 15-year period.

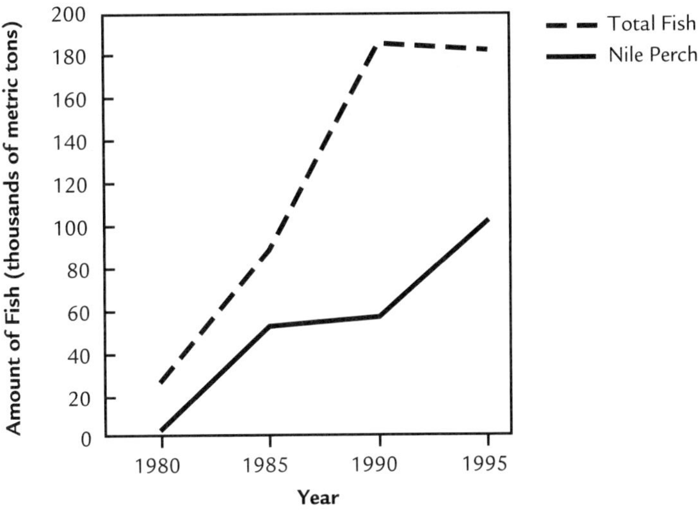

Figure 2: Amount of Fish Caught in Lake Victoria by Kenya

Besides increasing the amount of fish, there have been other consequences of introducing Nile perch into the lake. Because Nile perch are large and eat other fish, they are believed to have caused the extinction of as many as 200 species of cichlids. The populations of other types of fish, including catfish and lungfish, have also declined. Many ecologists are upset that their predictions have come true.

Some of the cichlids that have become extinct ate algae. With their extinction, the amount of algae in the lake has increased 5-fold. Algae use up a lot of oxygen, making it difficult for other tiny plants and animals to survive in the lake. Today, many of the deeper parts of the lake are considered "dead" because they don't contain much living matter.

However, many of the original goals have been met. In 1979, there were 16,000 fishermen along the Kenyan shores of the lake. In 1993, there were 82,300. Many people are now employed by companies that process and sell Nile perch overseas. Over time, these fish have brought more money into the African countries surrounding the lake. Local people, who now eat Nile perch as part of their diet, consider Nile perch a "savior."

Some ecologists wonder how long the current situation can last. Nile perch are predators. As populations of other fish decline, the Nile perch's food sources are declining. The stomachs of some large Nile perch have been found to contain smaller, juvenile Nile perch. What will happen to the population of Nile perch if their food supply dwindles even further? Will the Nile perch population be overfished like the fish populations before it? Only time will tell.

ANALYSIS

1. Based on the reading, how did the amount of fish caught in Lake Victoria change from the 1960s to 1989?

2. Based on Figure 2, describe how the amount of Nile perch caught by Kenya changed from 1980 to 1995.

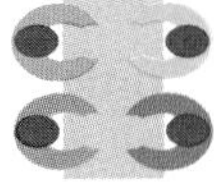

3. Look again at Figure 2. How do you think the number of metric tons of fish caught relates to the size of the total fish population from year to year? Explain your reasoning.

4. How did the introduction of Nile perch affect the food supply of the people who lived near Lake Victoria?

5. What effect did the introduction of Nile perch have on the organisms that lived in the lake?

6. Should Nile perch have been introduced into Lake Victoria? Support your answer with evidence and discuss the trade-offs of your decision.

   Hint: To write a complete answer, first state your opinion. Provide two or more pieces of evidence that support your opinion. Then consider all sides of the issue and identify the trade-offs of your decision.

7. What do you predict will happen to Lake Victoria over the next 20–30 years? Why?

73 Introduced Species

Introduced, non-native, exotic, and *non-indigenous* are all words used to describe species that humans have introduced outside of the species' normal range. The Nile perch is an **introduced species** that was placed deliberately into Lake Victoria. In other cases, the introduction of a new species into a new environment is accidental. Consider the case of the zebra mussel, which is named for the black and white stripes found on its shell. It was accidentally introduced into the United States in the 1980s and it is now estimated to cause up to $5 billion dollars of damage each year!

What effect can an introduced species have on an environment? What, if anything, should be done to control introduced species?

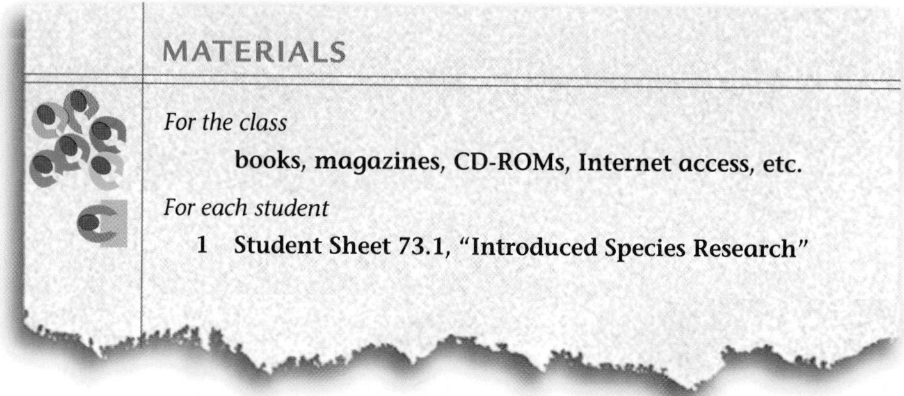

MATERIALS

For the class

books, magazines, CD-ROMs, Internet access, etc.

For each student

1 Student Sheet 73.1, "Introduced Species Research"

PROCEDURE

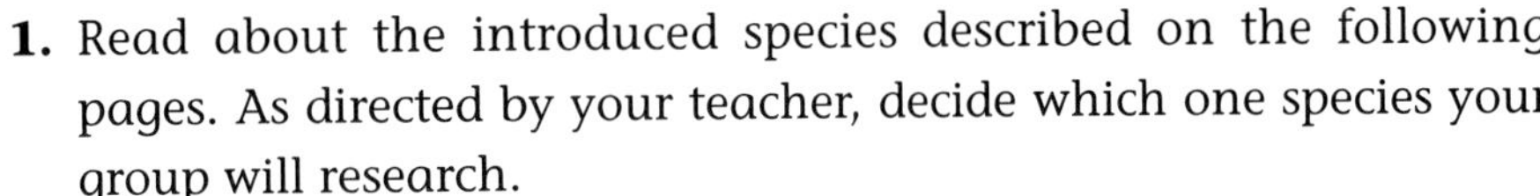

1. Read about the introduced species described on the following pages. As directed by your teacher, decide which one species your group will research.

2. Over the next few days or weeks, find information on this species from books, magazines, CD-ROMs, the Internet, and/or interviews. You can also go to the SALI page of the SEPUP website to link to sites with more information on species mentioned in this activity.
3. Use this information to complete Student Sheet 73.1, "Introduced Species Research." You should provide the following:
   - common and scientific name of your species
   - its native and current range; its relationship to and effect on people
   - its effect on new ecosystem(s)
   - the reasons for its success
   - issues related to its future growth or spread.

Later in this unit, you will use your research to create a class presentation.

EXTENSION

Visit a local greenhouse or botanical garden. Look at the labels of ornamental plants used in landscaping. Where did these plants originally come from? Is the introduction of these species considered to be good or bad?

Kudzu Brings Down Power Lines!

Kudzu (KUD-zoo), sometimes referred to as "the vine that ate the South," has finally pushed local patience to the limit. Properly called *Pueraria lobata,* it was first introduced in the 1920s to the southern United States as food for farm animals and to reduce soil erosion. Today, this fast-growing vine from Japan has overgrown entire forests and choked local ecosystems. Last week, the weight of kudzu vines pulled down power lines, causing a two-day power outage. Mayor Lam has called for control measures. All community members are invited to a town council meeting to consider what should be done to control this destructive vine.

Response to Tiger Mosquitoes Raises Questions

The public outcry over the worsening problem with the tiger mosquito *(Aedes albopictus)* continues. In response, the city has begun nighttime spraying of insecticide. Jesse Butler, principal of the Little Town Preschool, said, "How can the city be allowed to spray poison on the backyards where children play?" City spokesperson Kate O'Neil told reporters that the insecticide is harmless to people. "Tiger mosquitoes are very aggressive. They are much worse than the native mosquitoes. Apart from the nuisance, tiger mosquitoes can spread diseases such as yellow fever. We have to take action!" O'Neil invites interested residents to attend the Camford Mosquito Abatement Board presentation on the tiger mosquito problem and possible solutions.

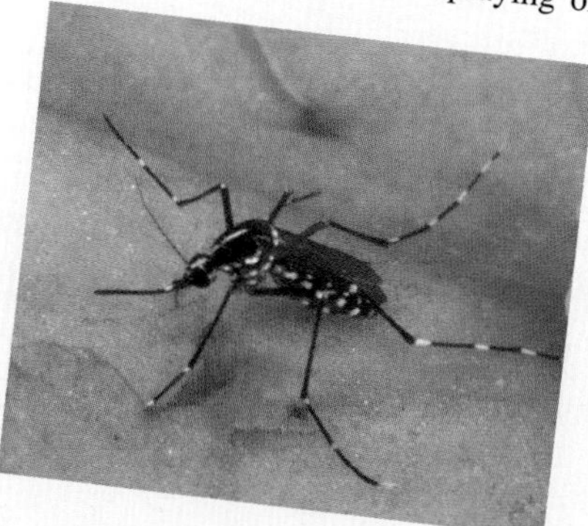

Nutria Hunting on State Marshes?

Ecologists from City University are considering teaming with local hunters in a surprise move to reduce the population of nutria (NEW-tree-uh) in state marshes. Nutria *(Myocastor coypus)* are large, beaver-like rodents whose burrows and voracious grazing are causing serious damage to marshes.

Ecologist Charlie Desmond told reporters that nutria are native to South America. They were brought to North America for their fur. When they escaped into the wild, their population exploded. "If we don't act soon, we could lose our marshlands in just a few years," he cautioned. Duck hunters, bird watchers, sport fishers, and hikers are pressuring the state legislature to come up with a solution. Nutria hunting is one option being seriously explored.

Aquarium Plant Turns Out to Be Worst Weed

You may have seen this aquatic plant sold in small bunches at aquarium stores. It's a popular plant because goldfish like swimming between its stems. But when aquariums are dumped out into lakes, ponds, or rivers, hydrilla (hie-DRILL-uh) can quickly grow into a dense mat that chokes out other vegetation. This change of the environment is dramatic for native animals and plants. *Hydrilla verticillata,* as it is known scientifically, can clog up city water intake valves and get tangled in boat propellers. "We used to have the best swimming hole down by the bridge," said Rita Aziz, a 7th grader at Junior Middle School. "Now it's filled with this gross weed. The last time I swam there, I got tangled in it. It was scary. I would really like to find a way to do something about it."

Cut Down Trees to Protect Them?

Agency Advises on Longhorn Beetle Threat

When Keesha Murray, age 3, was injured by a falling branch in Tot Play Park, local neighborhoods woke up to the threat of the Asian longhorn beetle. Her father, Toby Murray, said that Keesha had played under the big maple tree many times. Under the attack of the Asian longhorn beetle, the tree had recently died, which led to the loss of the tree limb. "Keesha was scratched up and scared. We were lucky it wasn't worse," he said.

Shade trees all over the city have been dying due to the recent invasion of this wood-boring beetle from Japan, known scientifically as *Anoplophora glabripennis*. The beetle larvae are very hard to kill. One suggestion is to cut down all trees within city parks to prevent the beetle from spreading.

A Landscape Beauty Is Taking Over

What is the link between landscaping your yard and the recent reports that local marsh species are declining? Purple loosestrife (*Lythrum salicaria*), whose magenta flowers are admired by gardeners, is the weed to blame. It was introduced from Europe as a medicinal herb in the early 1800s and is still sold today as a landscaping plant. According to the Fish and Wildlife Service ecologist Johanna Brown, "It totally takes over an area, crowding out native species. It's really devastating for fragile marsh ecosystems." Brian Van Horn, a teacher at Middleton Junior High, is also concerned. "It's a tough plant to get rid of and killing it can damage the marshes even more." A meeting at Middleton Junior High will be held to discuss this issue.

Farmers Rally to Scare Off Starlings

The recent outbreak of hog cholera may be related to starling *(Sturnus vulgaris)* droppings getting into pig food. Carol Polsky, a pig farmer in Poseyville, encouraged local farmers to work together to help get rid of the birds. "In addition to spreading disease, those birds eat crops, seeds, and animal feed. A flock of starlings will eat just about anything and they poop everywhere. That spreads disease to other animals, not just pigs," Polsky told reporters.

Many control options are available, according to Dr. Tony Caro of the Agricultural Sciences Board. Dr. Caro commented, "In 1891, 60 starlings were released in New York and now they are the most common bird in America!" But

a representative of the local nature society told reporters that the latest annual survey showed that starling populations had dropped since the previous year. Dr. Caro will be speaking at the next meeting of the County Farm Association, where control measures for starlings will be discussed.

Brown Snake Problem Bites Guam

Guam, a tiny, tropical island, is a U.S. territory with a problem. People have been bitten. Bird, bat, and lizard populations have declined. The culprit? The brown tree snake *(Boiga irregularis)* from New Guinea.

After baby Oscar Gonzalez was bitten by a brown tree snake, local people were spurred to action. "Most of us know about them. Those snakes climb the power poles and short out electricity on the island several times a week," Nicki DeLeon, a long-time resident of Guam, told reporters. "Back in the 1960s and even the 1970s, the jungle was full of birds singing. We used to see bats and little lizards running around. They're not so easy to find now."

Scientists are working to find ways to control the snake before the last of the unique island species disappear forever. Dr. Sheila Dutt, a researcher with EcoSave International, said, "As well as helping with snake control on Guam, we are desperate to prevent this snake from hitching a ride in air cargo. I don't even want to think of the effect this snake could have in other parts of the United States."

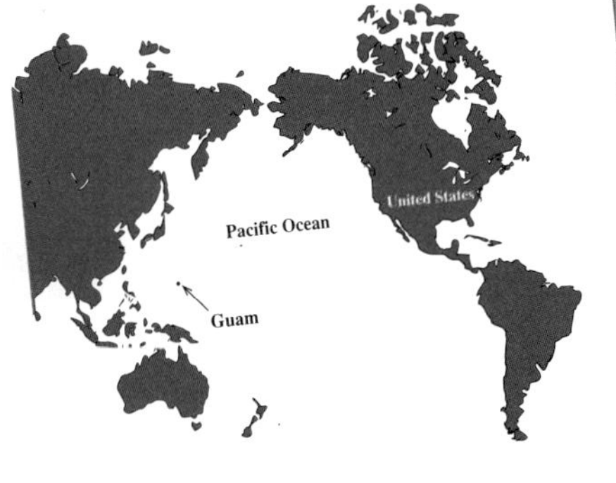

74 Observing Organisms

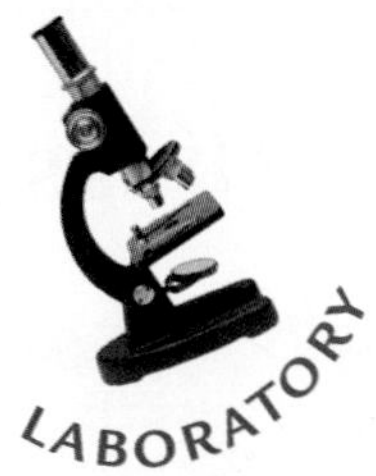

How do scientists know how introduced species affect ecosystems? Natural environments are constantly changing. How do you figure out what changes are due to the introduced organism and what changes are due to other factors? **Ecology** is the study of relationships between living organisms and the physical environment. Ecologists begin by studying organisms in the natural environment. They often supplement this information with laboratory investigations.

CHALLENGE

What can you discover about an organism in a laboratory investigation?

MATERIALS

For each pair of students

1 ***Lumbricculus variegatus*, or similar test organism**
1 **150-mm petri dish**
1 **piece of filter paper**
1 **pipet**
1 **small paintbrush**
1 **hand lens (optional)**
spring water (or treated tap water)

For the Extension

For the class

***Lumbriculus variegatus*, or similar test organisms**
pipets
microscopes
microscope slides

PROCEDURE

1. Pour 1–2 cm of water into the bottom of the petri dish.
2. Use the pipet to add a single blackworm from the culture to your petri dish. (Do not pick a blackworm that is dark and has a lighter section at one or both ends; this worm has recently been broken and is regenerating itself.)
3. Carefully observe the blackworm. Then use the brush to gently investigate this organism.
4. Record your observations. For example, how does the blackworm move? Does it respond differently to different actions, such as touching? Can you identify which end of the blackworm is the head? What else do you observe about the blackworm?
5. Place the filter paper in the lid of the petri dish. Use the pipet and a few drops of water to completely moisten the filter paper.

➢

6. Use the pipet to move the blackworm onto the filter paper.

7. Observe the blackworm's movement on this surface. How does its movement here compare with its movement in water? Record your observations.

8. Return your blackworm to the class culture before cleaning up.

EXTENSION

Place a blackworm on a microscope slide. Add one drop of water. (If there is too much water on the slide, use a pipet to suction off the excess water. Use your finger, not your mouth, to suction the water.) Observe the worm under low and medium power. What internal structures can you see?

ANALYSIS

1. Review your notes on how the blackworm responded to touch. How could these reactions help it to survive in the wild?

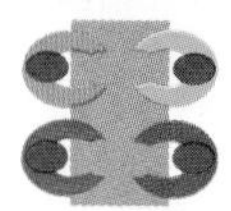

2. Based on what you now know about blackworms, in what type of environment do you think blackworms live? Explain your reasoning.

3. As an ecologist, you are asked to write an entry in an encyclopedia on the blackworm, *Lumbriculus variegatus.* Use your laboratory notes to write a paragraph describing the blackworm.

4. **a.** A student reading your encyclopedia entry thinks that you should include more information about blackworms. What questions do you think he or she might have after reading your entry?

   b. How might you get the information necessary to answer his or her questions?

75 Classifying Animals

There are many types of introduced species—just think about the differences between starlings and purple loosestrife! Most of the well-known cases belong to the plant or animal kingdom. While you may recognize kudzu, loosestrife, and hydrilla as plants, you may not have realized that all of the other introduced species discussed so far, including zebra mussels and tiger mosquitoes, are part of the animal kingdom. In fact, there are over one million known animal species in the world today, with many more being discovered every year. With such a large diversity of species, how do you know if the animal you are studying is similar to one another scientist is studying?

The five-kingdom classification scheme, shown in Figure 1, is one way of classifying species based on observations of their structures and other characteristics. This system helps scientists group species together to make sense of the diversity of life. It allows scientists to compare an organism, such as a zebra mussel, to other organisms with similar characteristics. In this activity, you will focus on organisms found in the animal kingdom.

The five-kingdom classification scheme is one of several ways scientists classify organisms. Other approaches to classification will be introduced in activities in the Evolution unit.

Figure 1: The Five-Kingdom Classification Scheme

Animals	Plants	Fungi	Protists	Bacteria

What are some similarities and differences among animals?

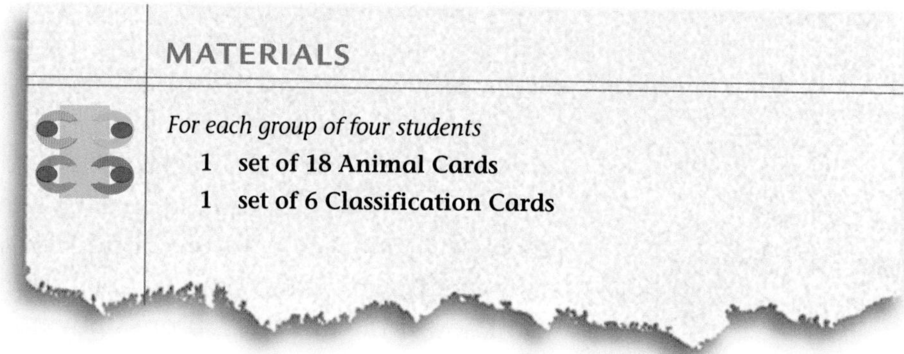

PROCEDURE

Part One: Exploring the Animal Kingdom

1. Spread your Animal Cards out on a table.
2. Look at each of the Animal Cards, noting similarities and differences among the animals.
3. Read the information on each card. This information represents what you might discover if you observed the animals more closely and were able to dissect a specimen.
4. With your student group, classify the animals into 4–8 groups. Work together to agree on a classification system:
   - If you disagree with others in your group about how to classify an animal, explain to the rest of the group why you disagree.
   - Listen to and consider other people's explanations and ideas.
5. In your science notebook, describe groups that you created: How many groups did you create? What do the animals in each group have in common? Be sure to record which animals you placed in which group.

6. Share your categories with another group of students. Explain why you classified the animals the way you did. Discuss how your group's categories were similar to or different from those of the other student group.

Part Two: A Biologist's Perspective

7. Spread out the Classification Cards on the table. (You may remember these cards from a previous *Science and Life Issues* activity.) Use the cards to review the characteristics of the five kingdoms and the non-living viruses.

8. Biologists use information similar to the descriptions provided on the Animal Cards to divide kingdoms into large categories called **phyla** (FIE-luh). The singular of *phyla* is *phylum*. Each phylum contains similar species. There are about 35 animal phyla. Your teacher will share with you how biologists group the animals on your cards into six of these phlya. Humans are grouped in the phylum Chordata, as shown below.

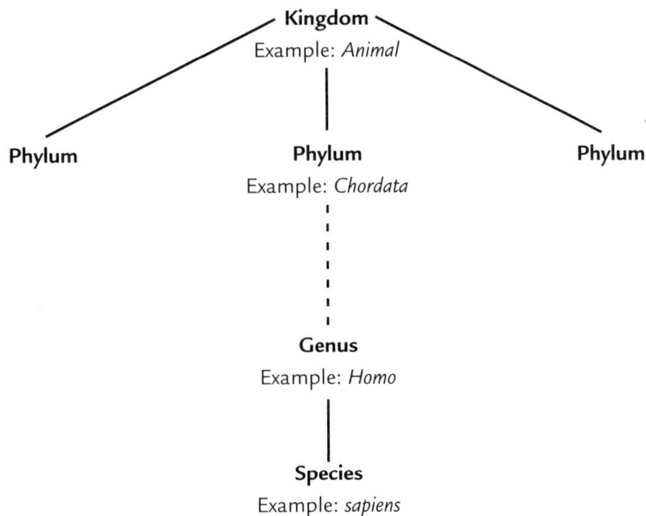

Humans are members of one of many phyla of animals.

9. Adjust your animal groups so they look like the phyla used by biologists today. Then complete Analysis Questions 1–3.

ANALYSIS

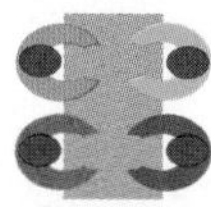

1. How did your categories change when you followed the biologists' system of phyla? Did your number of categories increase, decrease, or stay the same?

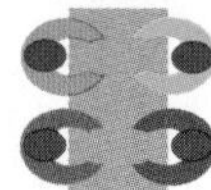

2. Look carefully at how biologists group these animals into phyla. What types of characteristics are used to group animals into phyla?

3. Animals without backbones are called invertebrates. How many invertebrate phyla do the animals on your Animal Cards represent? List these phyla.

4. **Reflection:** What characteristics were most important to you when you grouped the Animal Cards? How are these characteristics different from the ones that biologists use to classify? What do you now think is the best way to group animals? Explain.

76 People, Birds, and Bats

One of the 35 animal phyla—phylum Chordata—includes all species with backbones. Most of the chordates have a jointed backbone and are classified in the sub-phylum Vertebrata, or vertebrates. Although only about 50,000 vertebrate species have been identified (compared to about 1 million invertebrate species), the most familiar animals are vertebrates, such as humans, elephants, eagles, and frogs. How are vertebrates classified into smaller groups?

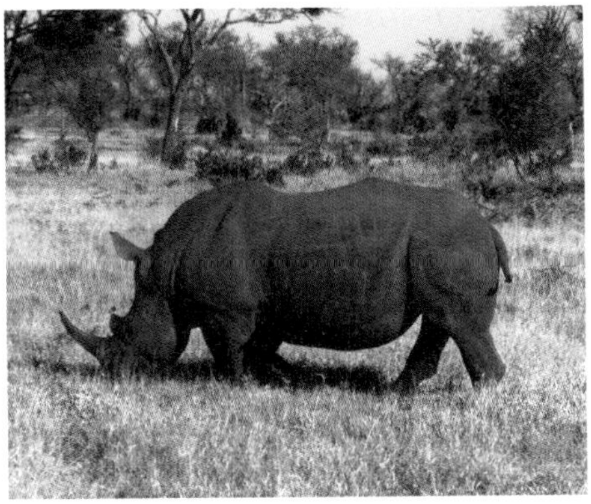

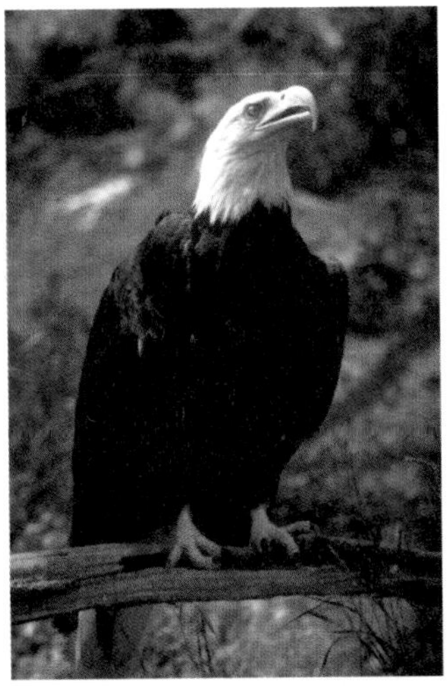

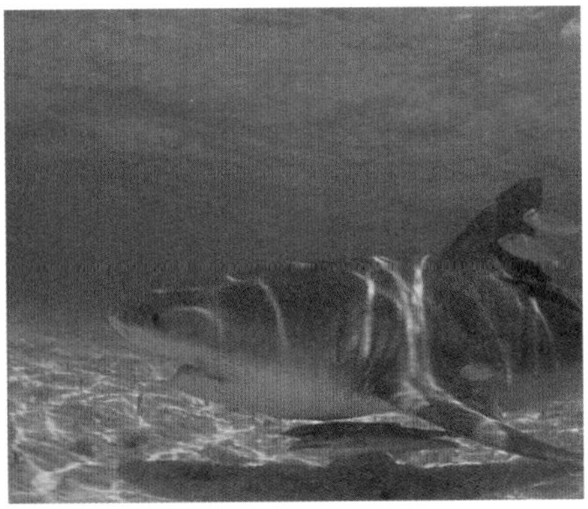

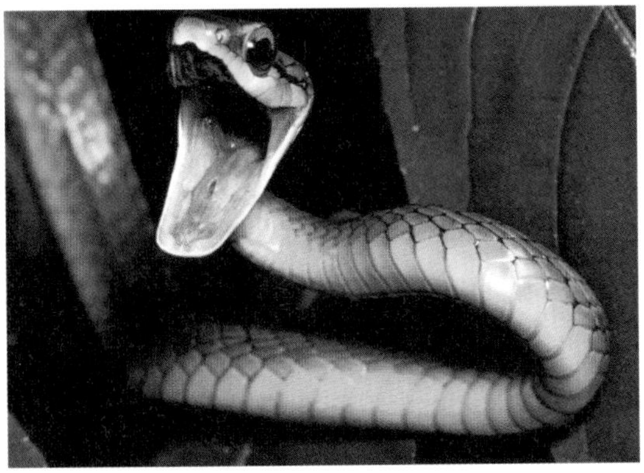

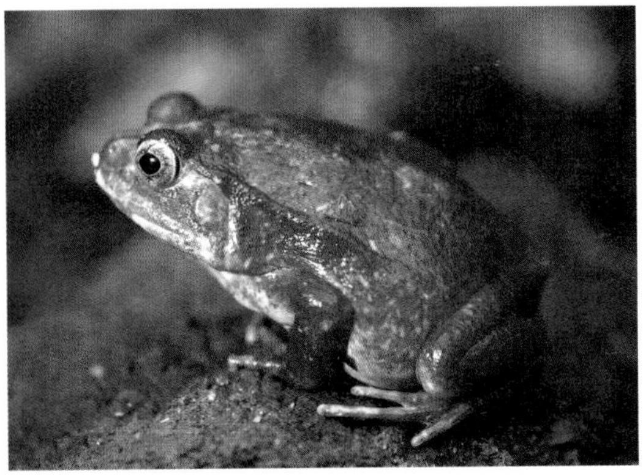

CHALLENGE

What kinds of evidence can you use to classify vertebrates?

PROCEDURE

1. Carefully read the Five-Kingdom Classification Chart on pages E30–E31 to compare characteristics of the five classes of vertebrates. "Cold-blooded" animals are animals that adjust their body temperature by moving to warmer or cooler locations. Their temperatures sometimes vary with the environment's temperature, but they aren't always cold. "Warm-blooded" animals regulate their body temperature to a fairly constant level by generating heat within their bodies, but they aren't always warm. Because of this, scientists now use different terms to describe these animals.

2. Pretend you work at a zoo. Some people have discovered some strange vertebrates and ask you for help in identifying them. They have sent you letters containing pictures and descriptions of these creatures. You can find the letters on pages E25–E29.

   For each mystery vertebrate:

   a. Read the letter and look at the picture.

   b. Discuss with your group members which vertebrate class might include this species.

   c. In your science notebook, record which class you believe it belongs to and your reasons. You do not need to agree with your group members.

ANALYSIS

1. What characteristics do you think best distinguish each vertebrate class?

2. Why do some vertebrates appear to fit into two or more different classes?

My husband and I were having lunch outside at our hotel in Mexico when I saw a small creature flash across the wall. I later saw a similar animal sunning itself outdoors. I'm enclosing a picture. The next day, I managed to catch one. It was sunning itself on a rock and its skin felt hot and dry, not moist. I could feel a line of bones along its back. As I held it, it seemed to get a little stressed; I noticed that it started to breathe faster. So I set it down and it ran off. We really liked these creatures and would like one as a pet. What kinds of animals are these?

J. Stirbridge

One of my kindergarten students brought in a picture of this animal. Hariette told the class that she saw one of these animals when she lived in New Zealand. She said that it looked hairy and that it was very rare. Harriette and her dad saw the animal poke around for worms with its sharp beak. Her dad is out of the country and Harriette wants to do a project on this animal. What is it? Thank You.

Mr. Kalmus and Class K-1

May 23, 1860

My collecting party was recently in the new territory of Australia, where we were astounded to find a most amazing variety of strange and unknown animals. The animal I have sketched below appears to be truly new to the world of science. We have also made observations of these creatures in their natural habitat. They live in ponds and streams and are covered by dark fur. The animal has a bill like a duck, which it uses to find snails and food in the mud of the stream. We then observed something most extraordinary. The female lays an egg which she keeps in her pouch until it hatches. The tiny baby licks milk from the skin of the mother's belly.

What is your opinion of these mysterious new creatures?

Sincerely,

Murray Jones

My girlfriend and I accidentally ran over this thing on our last road trip! Melia ran over to pick up the animal as soon as I stopped. The animal looked scaly, but had some hairs poking out between the "scales." Although it was a cold night, Melia said its body was still warm. Melia wants to put up signs warning people to look out for these animals so that no one else accidentally runs one over, but we don't know what they are. She's an artist, so she drew a picture of it for you. Can you help us identify this animal?

Tim

Nina and I are in 5th grade. We love to go snorkeling near the reefs by my house in Guam. We saw some very strange-looking animals underwater. I tried to draw one for you. They have a head like a horse but they have a fin on their back. One day, we saw one of them moving around and then some babies came out near its stomach! The babies swam straight to the surface but then came back down. We watched and watched but never saw them go back up to the surface. How can they breathe? What are they?

Thanks, Thomaso

➢

I was scuba diving in Thailand when I saw this long, striped creature, maybe as thick as my thumb, working its way along the bottom and sticking its head into holes. Its head was smaller than an eel's and I know that eels stay in their holes during the day. (This was a day dive.) Also, the animal was smooth and round, with no fins. I also noticed that it regularly went to the surface for air. Any ideas about what it is?

Phil

I am writing to ask you about some flying animals that nearly flew right into us when Pearl and I went caving last summer. We were near the entrance to a cave when I heard this twittering sound and saw some shadows fly past me. Pearl panicked and ran. She wouldn't go back to the cave. Later that night, I went exploring myself. When I shone my flashlight on the ceiling, I saw hundreds of really tiny animals hanging there. They seemed to be grouped together to keep warm because the cave was so cold. I think they were babies, because they looked much smaller than the creatures I had seen before. I saw one of the larger creatures fly into the cave and go to one of the babies. The baby seemed to be getting milk from the adult. I was wondering if you could help me figure out what these things are.

Sincerely yours,

Thelma

From: Ruby Riter

Subject: strange animal

I'm a travel writer with the Leisure Time Gazette. I was on assignment in Malaysia and saw these strange animals on the mud near mangrove swamps. I want to write about them for next week's travel section, but I need more information. I saw some of these animals swimming underwater, but I didn't see any of them come up for air. However, they seemed to do okay on land too. When I checked them out through a telephoto lens, I noticed that they had some kind of fin going down their back as well as scales on their bodies. Can you get back to me ASAP? My deadline is in three days. Thanks a lot.

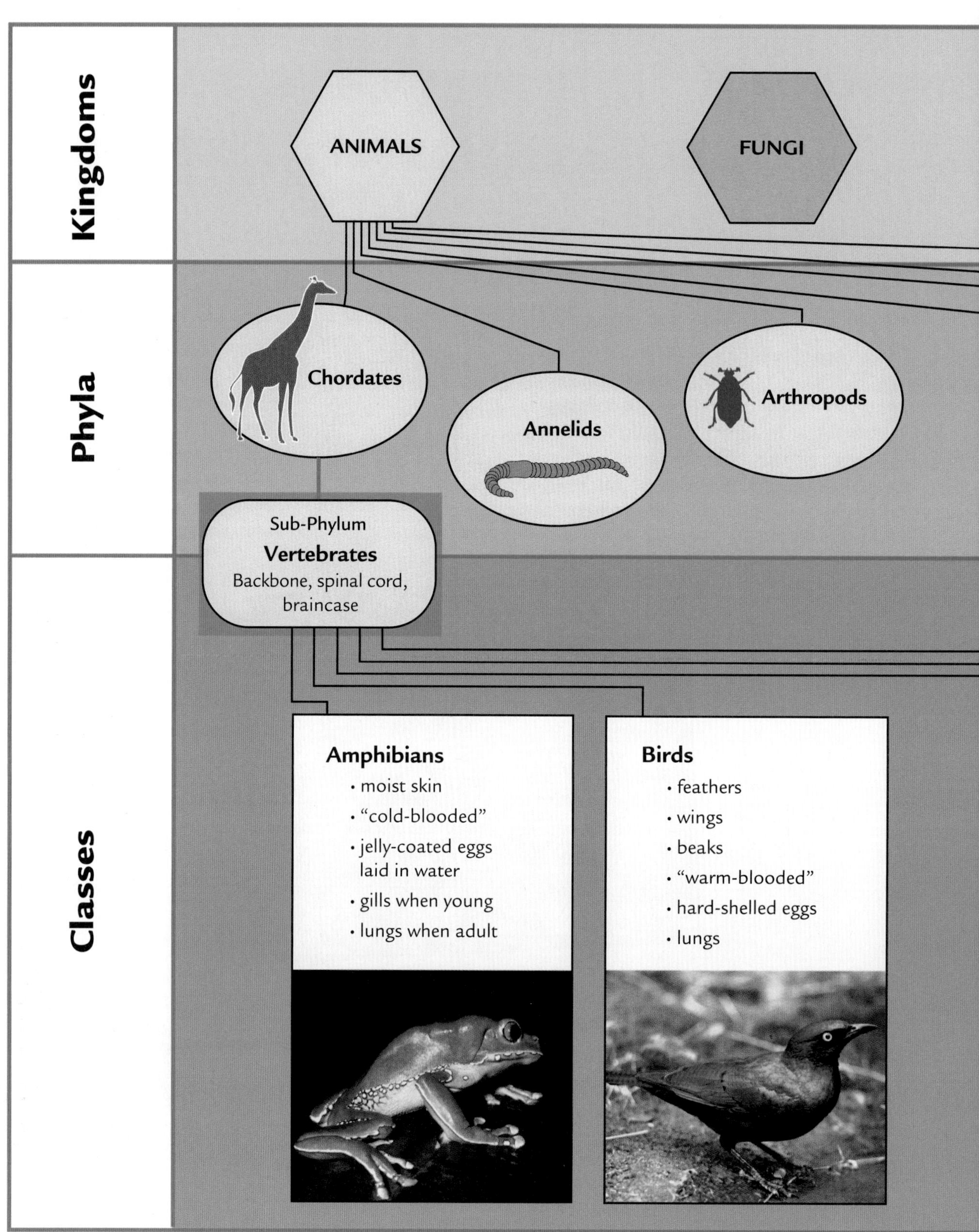
Kingdoms
ANIMALS
FUNGI
Phyla
Chordates
Annelids
Arthropods
Sub-Phylum
Vertebrates
Backbone, spinal cord, braincase
Classes
Amphibians
• moist skin
• "cold-blooded"
• jelly-coated eggs laid in water
• gills when young
• lungs when adult
Birds
• feathers
• wings
• beaks
• "warm-blooded"
• hard-shelled eggs
• lungs

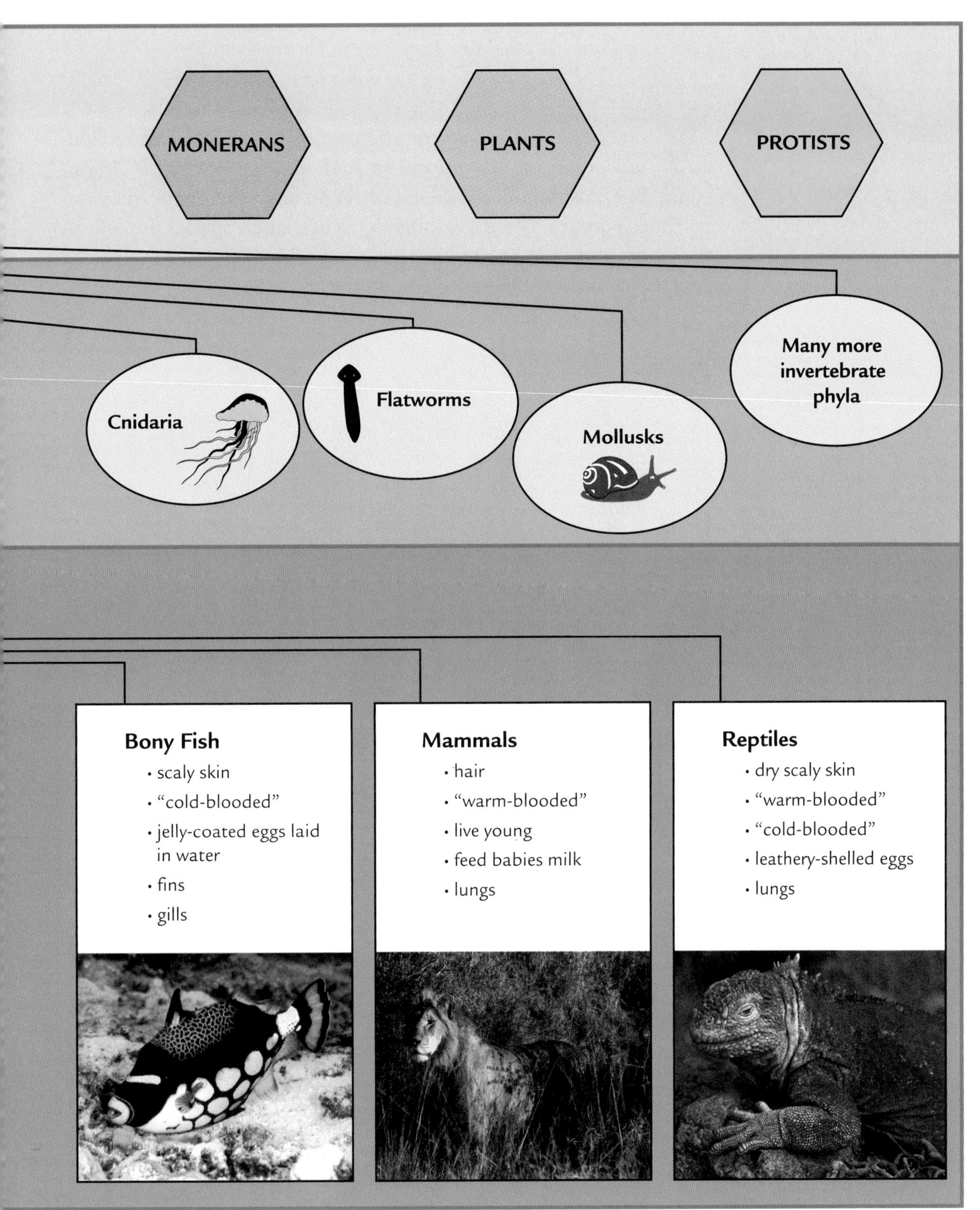
MONERANS
PLANTS
PROTISTS
Cnidaria
Flatworms
Mollusks
Many more invertebrate phyla
Bony Fish
• scaly skin
• "cold-blooded"
• jelly-coated eggs laid in water
• fins
• gills
Mammals
• hair
• "warm-blooded"
• live young
• feed babies milk
• lungs
Reptiles
• dry scaly skin
• "warm-blooded"
• "cold-blooded"
• leathery-shelled eggs
• lungs

77 Ups and Downs

You can gather ecological information by studying an individual organism, as you did in Activity 74, "Observing Organisms." But most organisms do not affect an environment as individuals, but as groups. Groups of individuals of a single species that live in the same place are known as populations. The photos on this page and the next show different populations of sea lions.

This population of sea lions lives on piers in a harbor.

One introduced species that is causing a lot of problems in the United States is the zebra mussel. Its success in freshwater environments has caused the loss of native wildlife as well as damage to equipment. How fast is this population spreading? Some investigators predict that populations of zebra mussels will be found across the entire United States within 20 years. Studying what has happened to populations of zebra mussels in lakes around the world can help scientists figure out what changes are occurring in the U.S. and what to expect for the future.

CHALLENGE

How do scientists study the size of a population and predict future population changes?

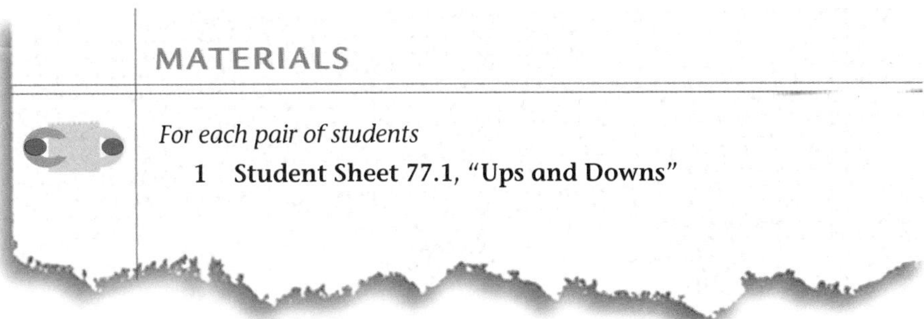

MATERIALS

For each pair of students

1 **Student Sheet 77.1, "Ups and Downs"**

This population of sea lions lives on a beach.

PROCEDURE

Part One: Initial Observations

1. In your group of four, review the two tables below. Imagine that two different groups of ecologists collected data on the size of the zebra mussel population in Lake Miko for two different time periods.

Table 1: Zebra Mussel Population in Lake Miko, Period 1 (1959 to 1968)

Year	1959	1960	1962	1968
Number of Zebra Mussels (per square meter)	2,211	95	93	97

Table 2: Zebra Mussel Population in Lake Miko, Period 2 (1971 to 1976)

Year	1971	1972	1974	1976
Number of Zebra Mussels (per square meter)	393	802	1,086	2,179

2. Divide your group in half. Assign one of the two data tables to each pair within your group.

3. With your partner, create a line graph of the data in your table using Student Sheet 77.1, "Ups and Downs." Remember, independent variables, such as time, are always graphed on the x-axis. Since you will compare graphs within your group, make sure that the x-axes of both graphs use the same scale.

4. After completing your graph, respond to the two questions on Student Sheet 77.1 as directed.

Part Two: A More Complete Analysis

5. Show your graph to the other students in your group. Point out the overall population trend—is the population increasing, decreasing, or staying the same?

6. Compare the two graphs. Discuss what conclusions you can make about the population trend in Lake Miko during Period 1 vs. Period 2.

7. Place the two graphs together, with the graph for Table 1 first and the graph for Table 2 second. If necessary, fold the edges of your sheets to fit the graphs together.

8. As a group, discuss what happens to the population trends when the two graphs are connected. Discuss how what you see with the two graphs together is different from what you see with each of the individual graphs. Be sure to:

   - Describe what happens to the population size of zebra mussels in Lake Miko from 1959–1976.

   - Discuss whether you can make any definite conclusions about whether the population is increasing, decreasing, or staying the same.

ANALYSIS

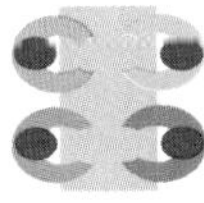

1. **a.** Sketch a line on your graph predicting what you think will happen to the size of this population of zebra mussels during the ten years after 1976.

   b. Explain your prediction. Why do you think the graph will look that way?

   c. What additional information would make you more confident of your prediction? Explain.

2. **a.** What factors do you think affect the size of a population?

   b. Explain how each factor might affect population size: Would it cause the population to increase, decrease, or stay the same? Why?

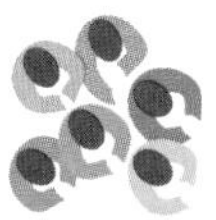

3. As you know from your own graph, data were not collected every year. Explain whether you would expect a well-designed experiment to collect data every year. What might prevent the collection of such data?

4. Shown below are graphs of zebra mussel populations in three lakes near Lake Mikolajskie. Describe the population trend in each graph. How does each population change over time?

Zebra Mussel Populations in Three Lakes

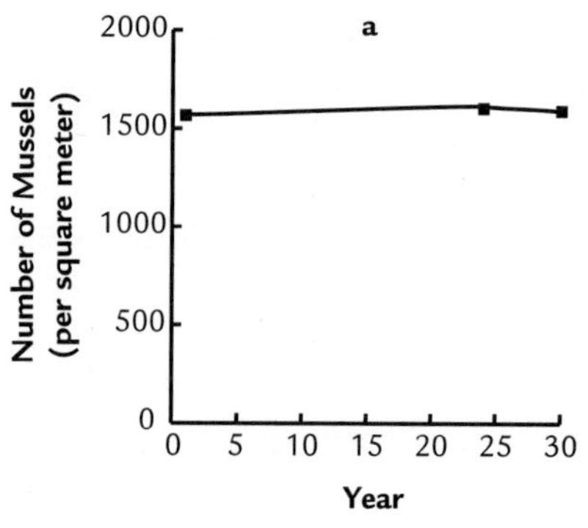

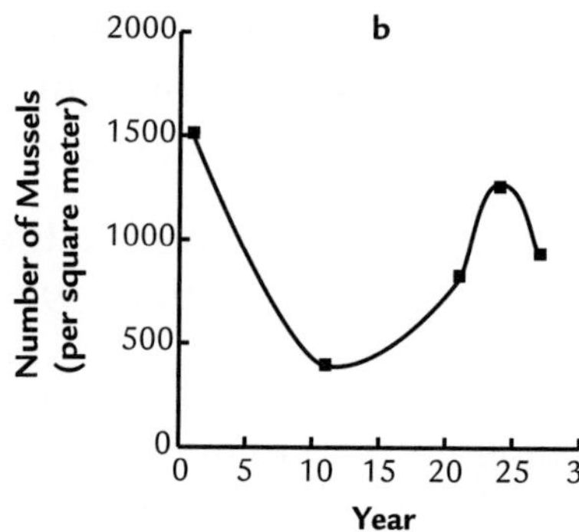

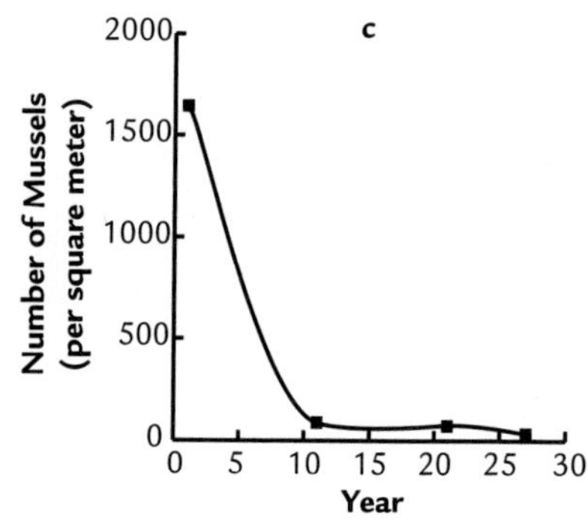

5. The data presented in this activity are similar to actual data collected in Lake Mikolajskie, Poland, between 1959 and 1987. Zebra mussels have been found in lakes in that area for over 150 years. Shown below are the data collected from 1977–87. How does this additional information compare to your answer to Question 1?

Table 3: Zebra Mussel Population in Lake Miko, Period 3 (1977 to 1987)

Year	1977	1979	1982	1983	1987
Number of Zebra Mussels (per square meter)	77	104	81	55	85

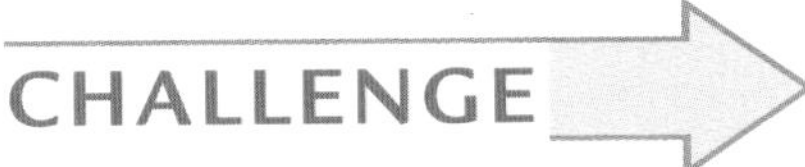

CHALLENGE

What can an owl pellet tell you about an owl's diet? How can you use this information to develop part of a food web?

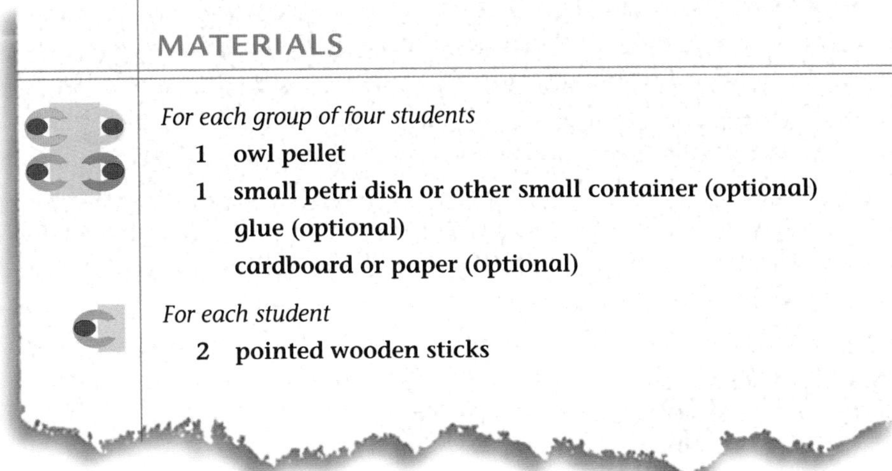

MATERIALS

For each group of four students

1 **owl pellet**
1 **small petri dish or other small container (optional)**
glue (optional)
cardboard or paper (optional)

For each student

2 **pointed wooden sticks**

PROCEDURE

1. Use the wooden sticks to carefully pull the owl pellet into four equal-sized pieces. Provide each member of your group with one of the four pieces.
2. Use your pair of sticks to gently separate all of the bones from the fur of your piece of owl pellet.
3. Work with your group to divide all of the bones into groups based on their shapes. Use Table 1, "Guide to Owl Pellet Bones," to help you.
4. Count and record the number of bones in each of your categories.
5. Try to arrange the bones to make a skeleton of one (or more) animal. Sketch your final arrangement(s).

Table 1: Guide to Owl Pellet Bones	
Skulls	
Jaws	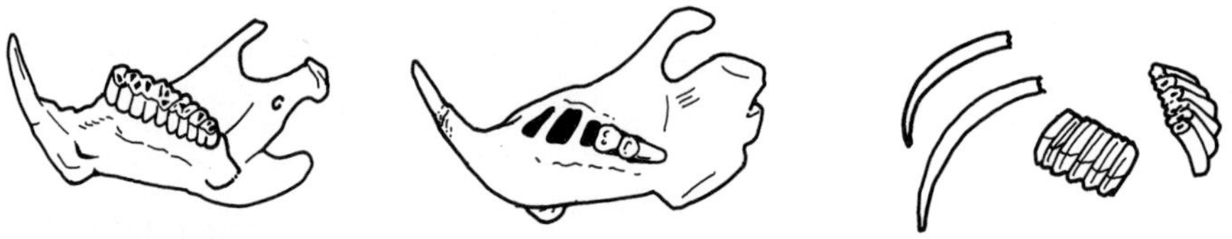
Shoulder blades	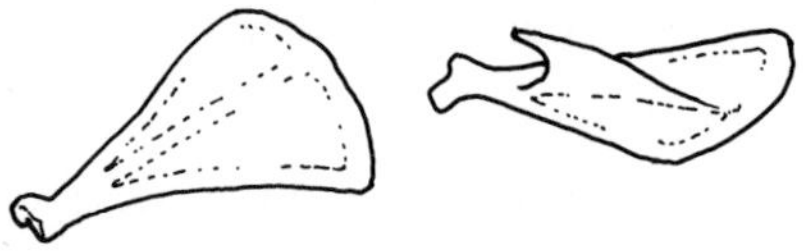
Front legs	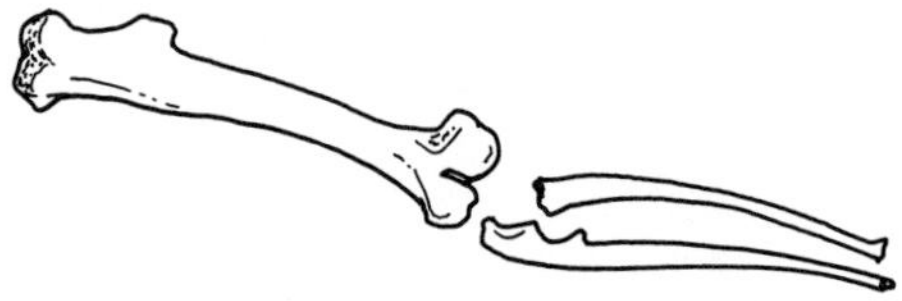
Hips	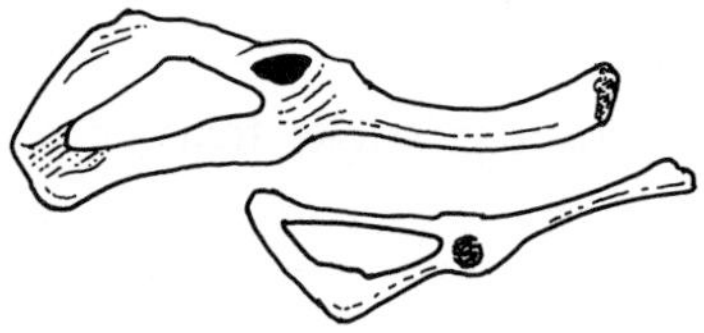
Hind legs	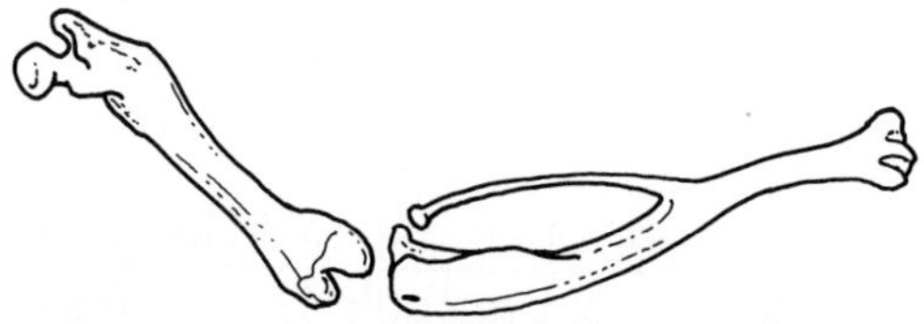
Assorted ribs	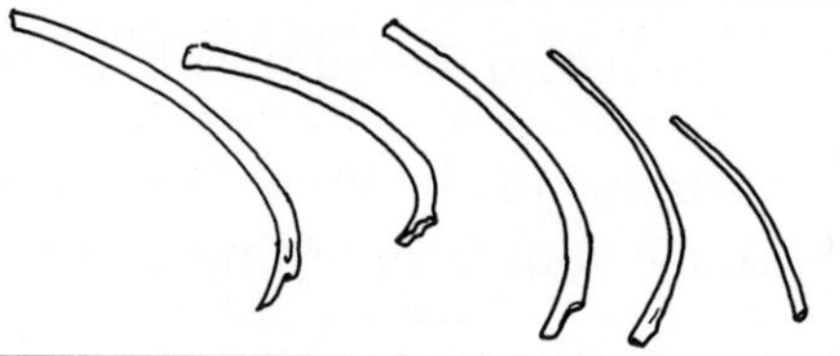
Assorted vertebrae	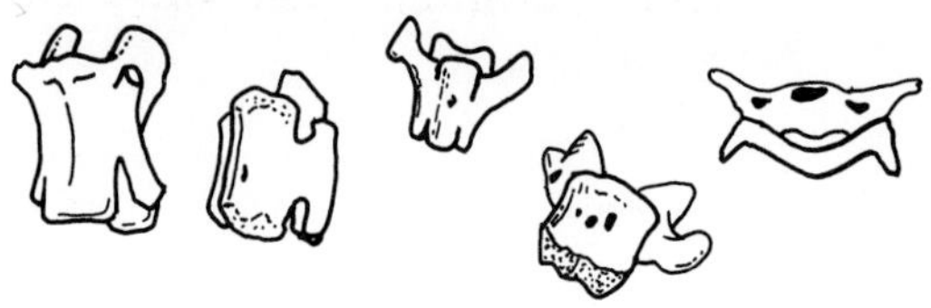

ANALYSIS

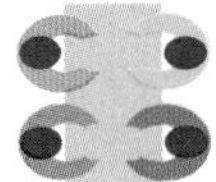

1. What did you learn about the diet of owls from investigating an owl pellet? Include information about the type and number of organisms in an owl's diet. (Remember that an owl ejects a pellet within 12 to 24 hours after eating.)

2. **a.** The organisms that you uncovered in your owl pellet are likely to be voles, small rodents similar to mice. Owls also eat other small mammals, such as shrews, and insects. Use this information on owl diet to develop a food web.

   b. Voles eat mostly plant material such as grass, seeds, roots, and bark. Shrews eat insects. Add these relationships to your food web.

   c. The great horned owl sometimes eats other owls. It also eats small mammals like voles. Add the great horned owl to your food web.

3. Copy the graph shown below, which is similar to graphs you made in Activity 77, "Ups and Downs." It predicts the change in the population of owls as they first move into a new habitat.

Owl Population Over Time

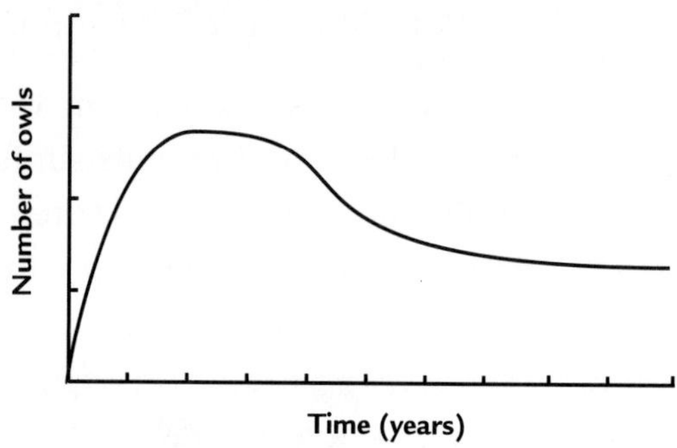

a. Draw a line showing what you think will happen over the same time period to the population of one of the species that owls eat.

b. Draw a line, using a different color or symbol, showing what you think might happen over the same time period to the population of one of the species that eats owls. Be sure to include a key identifying what species each line represents.

EXTENSION

Research the food web of the introduced species you are studying. What effects, if any, has your species had on native species? What effects do you predict it will have in the future?

79 Eating for Energy

One important part of every organism's habitat is a source of food. The introduction of new species into an **ecosystem** often changes the availability of food.

How are the energy relationships among organisms in an ecosystem affected by the introduction of a new species?

READING

Is it possible that a scenario like the one in Lake Victoria could happen in the United States? Scientists are waiting to see. But in the United States, the main concern isn't a large predator like the Nile perch, but a seemingly unimportant mussel less than two inches long. The tiny zebra mussel *(Dreissena polymorpha)* (see Figure 1) doesn't seem large enough to cause serious problems. But its ability to reproduce and spread quickly is making it into a big issue.

Figure 1: Zebra Mussels Feeding

Zebra mussels reproduce by releasing eggs and sperm into the water. The fertilized eggs grow into tiny larvae. Because of their small size, they are very hard to see at this stage.

STOPPING TO THINK 1

Brainstorm ways in which zebra mussels might accidentally be spread from one lake to another.

Zebra mussels feed on some of the smallest members of the aquatic food chain: microscopic animals and plants known as **plankton** (PLANK-tun) (see Figure 2). (When discussing them in more detail, biologists usually use the words *zooplankton* [zoe-uh-PLANK-tun] for microscopic animals and *phytoplankton* [fie-toe-PLANK-tun] for microscopic plants.) Plankton are found throughout the water, from the very deepest part of a lake to the surface. They are the food for a variety of other organisms, including many kinds of fish. In addition, zooplankton eat phytoplankton. Thus, phytoplankton are at the base of many aquatic food chains.

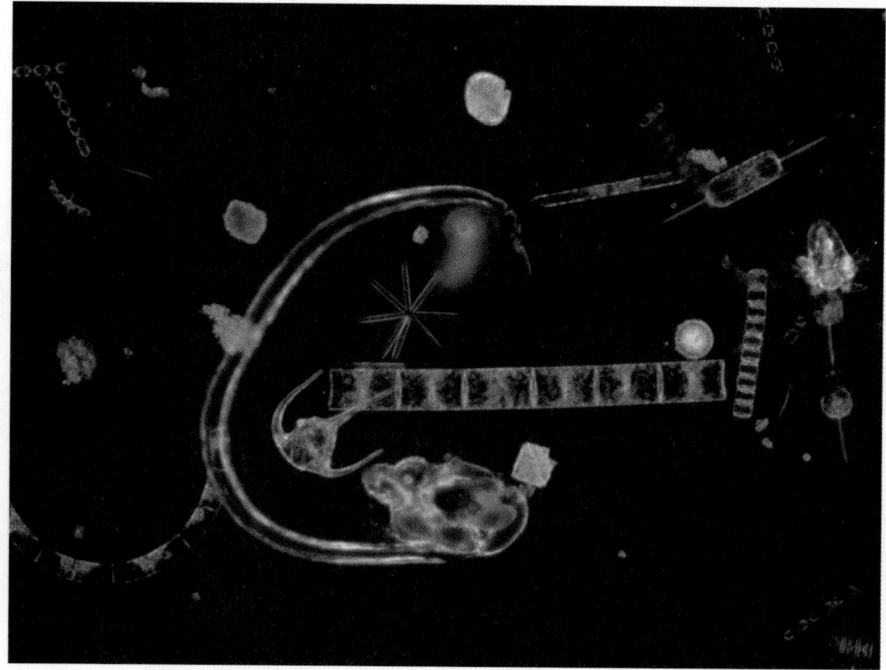

Figure 2: Plankton

Phytoplankton include microscopic plants and algae. These tiny organisms are especially important in aquatic ecosystems because they produce food for all the other living things in that ecosystem. You may know that plants and algae require sunlight in order to grow. They use sunlight as energy to convert carbon dioxide and water into food—a process known as **photosynthesis** (foe-toe-SIN-thuh-sis). (You will learn more about photosynthesis in Activity 81, "A Producer's Source of Energy.") The food that the plant produces is stored within the plant as starch or sugar. The plant can then use its food for activities within its own cells—until the plant is eaten by another organism! Since most plants and algae do not eat other organisms for food but are able to produce their own food, they are called **producers**. Producers such as phytoplankton form the base of the food chain because they have the ability to use the sun's energy to make their own food.

All other organisms rely on this ability of producers to convert the energy from the sun into food energy. Organisms that get their energy by eating food are known as **consumers**. Some consumers eat plants for energy, while other consumers eat the animals that eat plants. Some consumers, such as zebra mussels and humans, eat both plants and animals.

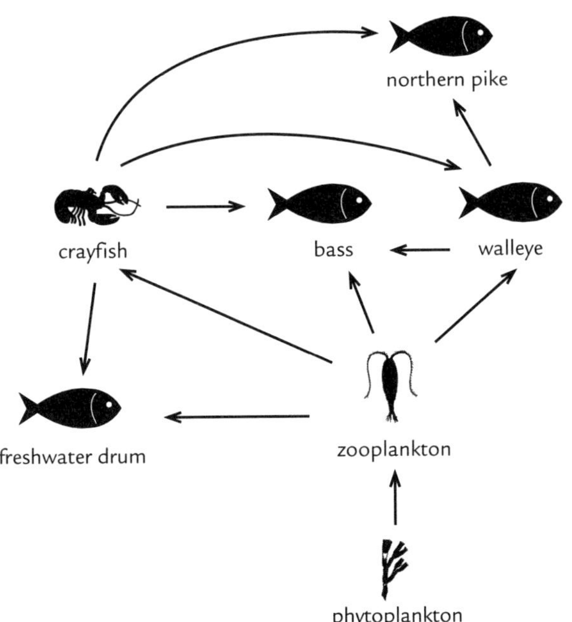

Figure 3: A Simplified Lake Food Web

STOPPING TO THINK 2

Why are producers, such as plants, an essential part of any ecosystem?

In Figure 3, you can see a simplified lake food web with both producers and consumers. The transfer of energy that takes place when one organism eats another is shown by arrows. Each arrow shows where the energy from the food is going within the ecosystem. The arrows show who is eaten by whom, not who eats whom. Many other species eat phytoplankton; food webs become more complicated when additional relationships are added.

STOPPING TO THINK 3

a. Copy Figure 3 into your science notebook. Identify each organism as either a producer or a consumer.

b. Think about the kinds of food that people eat. Use this knowledge to add humans into this lake food web.

c. In the lake food web, humans are consumers. Are humans always consumers? Explain.

After zebra mussels appeared in the Great Lakes ecosystem, they changed the food web. Zebra mussels filter water and catch the microscopic plankton that live in the water. They rely on phytoplankton and zooplankton for food. Because zebra mussels are often more common than other sources of food, crayfish and freshwater drum are starting to eat zebra mussels as part of their diet.

STOPPING TO THINK 4

Using Figure 3 as a guide, create a lake food web that includes zebra mussels. Be sure to show how zebra mussels get their energy *and* how other organisms get energy from them.

At first, these changes don't seem too important. After all, couldn't the lake ecosystem support one more consumer? Adult zebra mussels filter about one liter of water per day. This means that a two-inch mussel can filter enough water to fill half of a large soft drink bottle every day. In some parts of the Great Lakes, the concentration of zebra mussels has reached as high as 70,000 mussels in a square meter. This means that just a small area of mussels would be able to filter 70,000 liters of lake water each day! As a result of zebra mussels, the clearness of the water has changed: it is now 600% clearer than it was before the introduction of the zebra mussels. Clear water sounds like a good thing, but biologically speaking, extremely clear water can mean that there is not much alive in the water. In fact, the zebra mussel population has been so effective at filtering plankton that the populations of some types of phytoplankton have decreased by 80%.

Remember, phytoplankton are the base of this aquatic food chain. By removing large amounts of phytoplankton from the water, zebra mussels remove the food for microscopic zooplankton. Many types of fish depend on zooplankton for food. In some cases, these fish are the food for other fish and for humans and other mammals. Some ecologists predict that zebra mussels will change the entire food web of the lake ecosystem. However, there is no evidence yet that zebra mussels have affected fish populations in the lake.

There is evidence, though, that the types of plants in the lake are changing. Because of the increased clearness, sunlight is now able to penetrate deeper into the lake. Plants such as algae are now growing along the lake bottom. This provides habitat and food for other organisms, such as sunfish, that are currently not common in the lake. Some scientists predict that the fish populations will change: populations of some fish, like walleye, will decrease, while populations of other fish, like sunfish, will increase.

What will happen to the lake ecosystem? At this point, no one is sure. The one thing that everyone is sure of is that zebra mussels will spread. The dots in Figure 4 mark areas where the zebra mussel is now found.

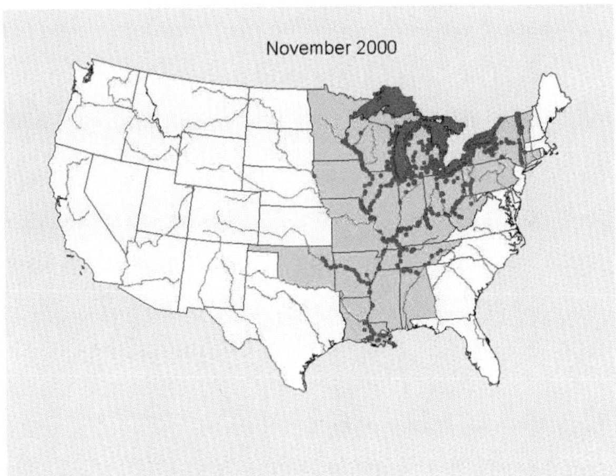

Figure 4: Spread of Zebra Mussels Across the United States

STOPPING TO THINK 5

Look at Figure 4: the lines across the U.S. represent large rivers. Where do you predict zebra mussels will be found in the next 10 years? The next 20 years? The next 50 years? Explain your predictions.

EXTENSION

Go the SALI page of the SEPUP website to link to the website of the United States Geological Survey. What is the current status of zebra mussel spread across the U.S.?

ANALYSIS

1. A volcano erupts 40 miles from the lake ecosystem whose food web you drew in Stopping to Think 4. Ash from the eruption blocks sunlight over your ecosystem for several months. Explain what happens to each population within the lake food web in the weeks that follow the eruption.

2. The ash clears and several more months go by. Think about what is now happening to your lake ecosystem. Identify what factors will affect how quickly it recovers.

3. **Reflection:** Think about what you have learned about introduced species as well as ecosystems. What effect(s) can an introduced species have on an ecosystem?

80 Nature's Recyclers

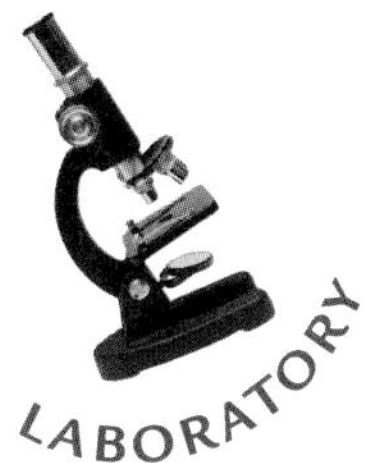

You have learned about the roles of producers and consumers in a food web. But what about worms, bacteria, and fungi? What role do they play within an ecosystem? Organisms that eat dead organisms and wastes from living organisms are known as **decomposers.** Worms, bacteria, and fungi are decomposers. You can think of decomposers as a special type of consumer: they consume dead organisms and waste material.

Fungi such as these decompose wood and other dead plant material.

Decomposers like worms and bacteria can seem unimportant. The decay they cause can look (and smell) horrible. But decomposers are essential to the ability of ecosystems to recycle important nutrients like carbon and nitrogen. Decomposers like bacteria and fungi break down dead matter into chemicals that can be absorbed by plants. Without decomposers, dead organisms would pile up and the nutrients they contain could not be re-used by plants. Eventually, the fertility of soil and aquatic ecosystems would be reduced to nothing. Imagine what the bottom of a lake would look like without any decomposers!

➢

Where can you find some decomposers? What do these decomposers look like?

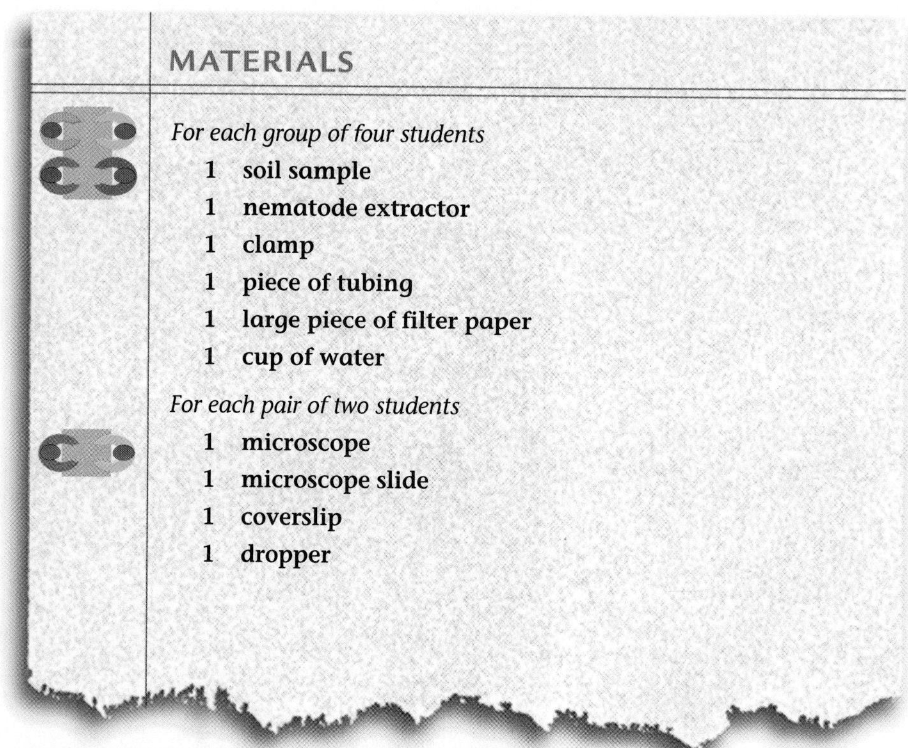

MATERIALS

For each group of four students

- 1 soil sample
- 1 nematode extractor
- 1 clamp
- 1 piece of tubing
- 1 large piece of filter paper
- 1 cup of water

For each pair of two students

- 1 microscope
- 1 microscope slide
- 1 coverslip
- 1 dropper

PROCEDURE

Part One: Investigating Soil

1. Gather ½ cup of soil from outdoors by scraping or shaking moist soil from around the roots of a clump of grass or other plant or from an area of decomposing leaf litter.
2. Place the tubing on the spout of the funnel. Then attach the clamp onto the middle of the tubing, as shown in Figure 1. Make sure that the tubing is pushed as far as it can go into the clamp; otherwise the water can drip out.

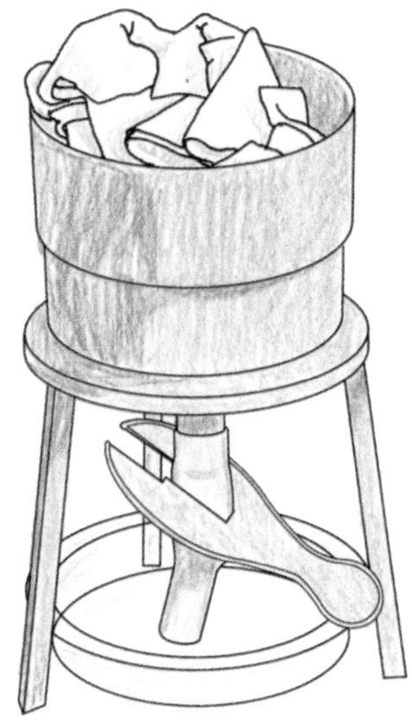

Figure 1: Nematode Extractor

3. Place the funnel in the stand and the perforated disc into the funnel.

4. Add water to the funnel to the level of the perforated disc.

5. Place the piece of filter paper in the funnel. Add a layer of your soil sample, no more than 1 cm deep, onto the filter paper.

6. Fold the filter paper over the soil. Add just enough water to cover the soil and filter paper. Set aside for one day.

Part Two: Searching for Nematodes

7. Carefully remove the clamp to release a small amount (less than 5 mL) of water into the cup. Share this sample in your group of four.

8. You might be able to see some small, white thread-like objects in the water. Try to suck up one of the thread-like objects into the dropper. Then squeeze a couple of drops from the dropper onto a microscope slide.

9. Carefully touch one edge of the coverslip, at an angle, to the mixture. Slowly allow the coverslip to drop into place.

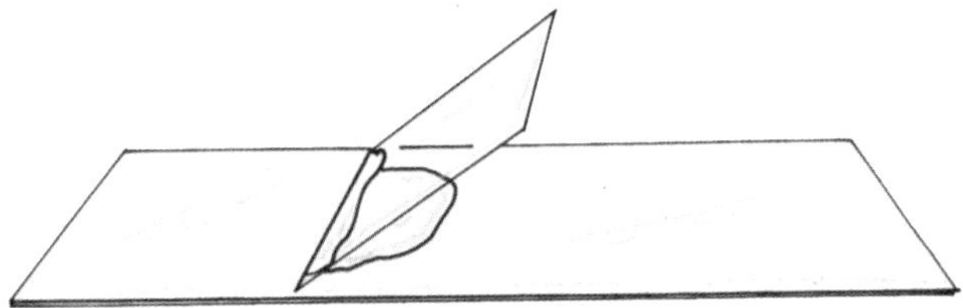

10. Begin by observing the slide on low power (usually the 4x objective). Be sure that the sample is in the center of the field of view (you may need to move the slide slightly) and completely in focus before going on to the next step.

Hint: To check that you are focused on the sample, move the slide slightly while you look through the eyepiece—the sample that you are focused on should move as you move the slide.

11. Without moving the slide, switch to medium power (usually the 10x objective). Adjust the microscope settings as necessary.

Hint: If material on the slide is too dark to see, increase the amount of light on the slide: do this by slightly opening the diaphragm under the stage.

➢

12. While looking through the eyepiece, move the slide around slowly so that you see all parts of your sample. As you scan the slide, look for movement, especially of thin, colorless organisms like the ones shown in Figure 2. These organisms look like small earthworms, but are actually members of a different phylum. These tiny worms are called nematodes (NEM-uh-toads). (If you do not find any nematodes on your slide, make another slide from your sample.)

13. Try to count the number of nematodes on your slide. Compare the number of nematodes you and your partner find with the rest of your group.

14. When you have completed your observations, turn off the microscope light and set the microscope back to low power.

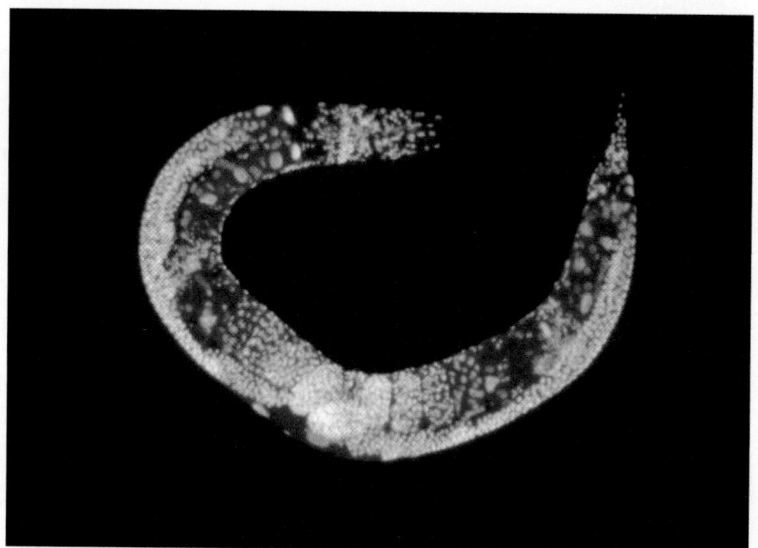

Figure 2: A nematode

ANALYSIS

1. Think about where some nematodes are found. What do you think they eat? Describe the role of nematodes in the ecosystem.

2. a. A simplified food web is shown on the next page. Which of the organisms in this ecosystem are producers? Which are consumers? Which are decomposers?

   b. Use the food web to explain why decomposers could be considered a special type of consumer.

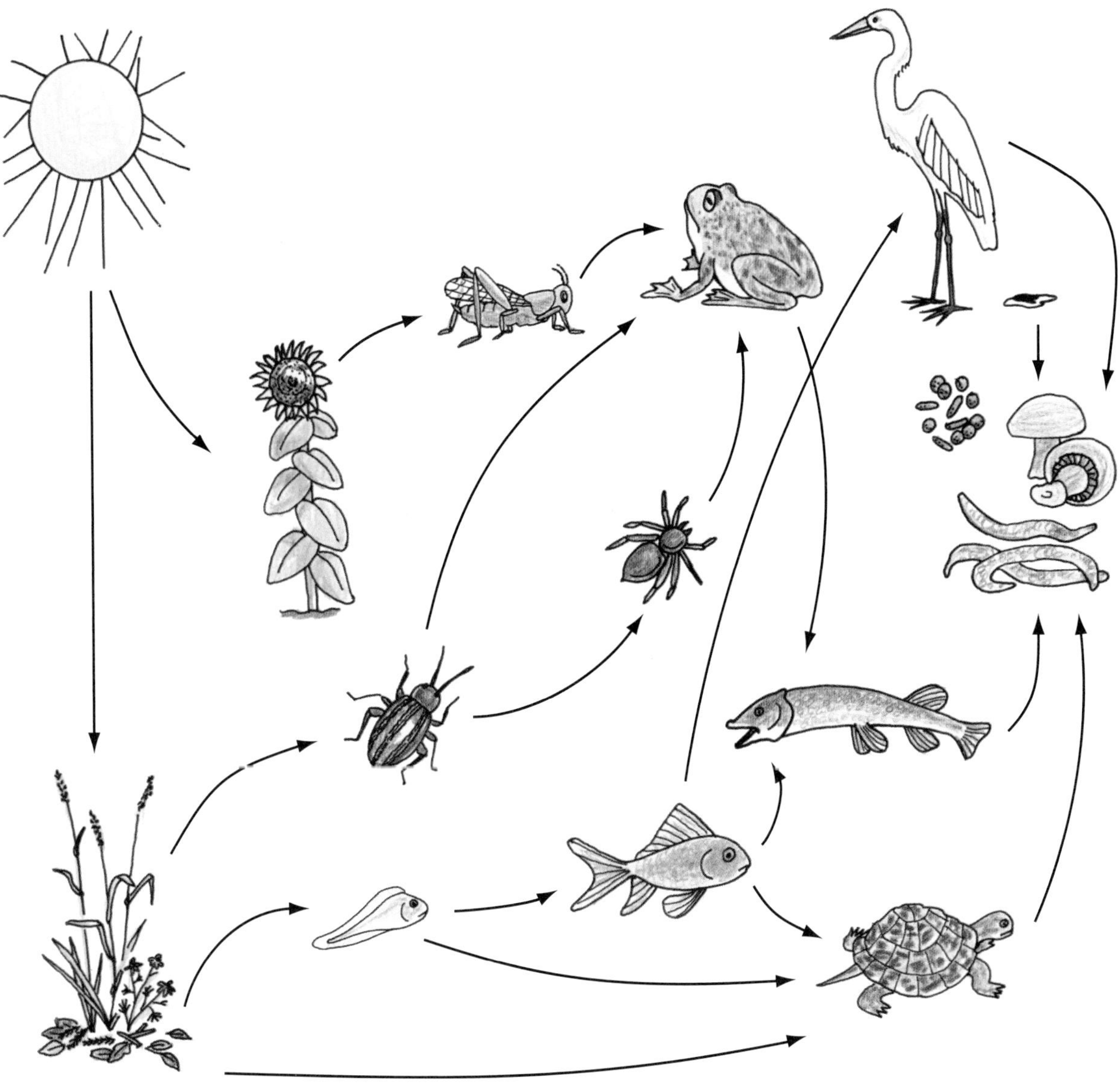

3. Like all organisms, birds like the egret need energy to live. Explain how the original source of energy for egrets, and all other consumers, is the sun.

4. Imagine that something kills most of the bacteria and other decomposers in a lake. What are some possible effects of killing these decomposers?

81 A Producer's Source of Energy

Producers such as phytoplankton and plants provide the energy for all other living creatures—for the consumers that eat plants, the consumers that eat animals that eat plants, and the decomposers that live off dead plants and animals. They do this by means of photosynthesis, a process by which plants use the energy from sunlight to convert carbon dioxide and water into food for themselves (and indirectly, for consumers). During this process, plants release oxygen gas into the atmosphere. Photosynthesis can be described by the following word equation:

$$\text{carbon dioxide} + \text{water} \xrightarrow{\textit{sunlight}} \text{food} + \text{oxygen}$$

Is light necessary for photosynthesis? How important is sunlight to an ecosystem? In this activity, you will use the indicator bromthymol blue (BTB) to collect evidence for the role of light in photosynthesis.

How do scientists study the role of light in photosynthesis?

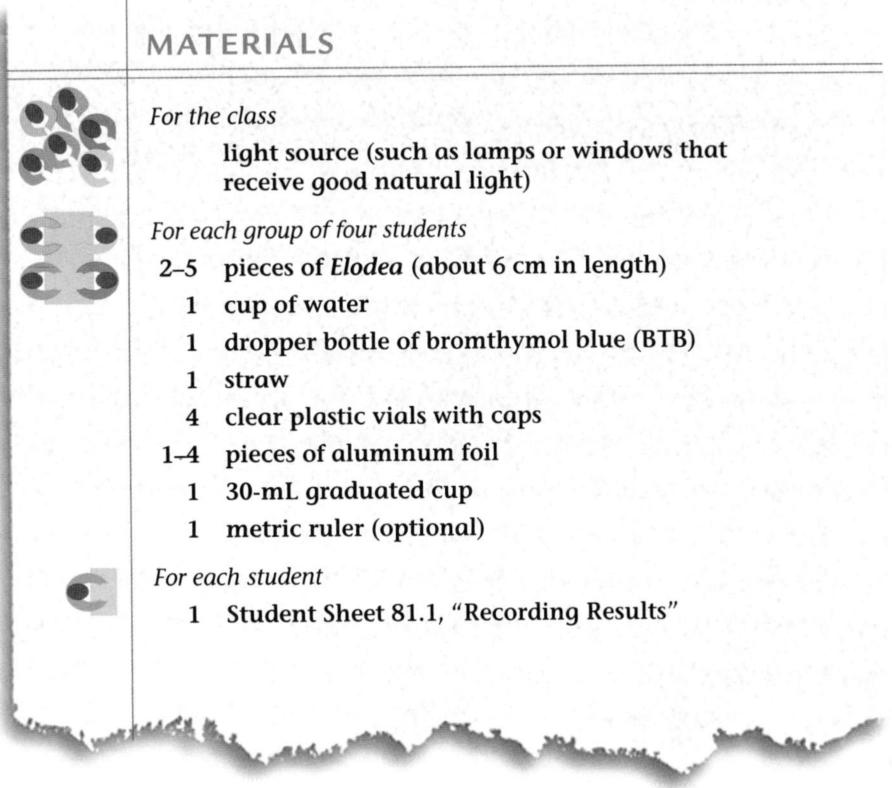

MATERIALS

For the class

light source (such as lamps or windows that receive good natural light)

For each group of four students

2–5 pieces of *Elodea* (about 6 cm in length)

1 cup of water

1 dropper bottle of bromthymol blue (BTB)

1 straw

4 clear plastic vials with caps

1–4 pieces of aluminum foil

1 30-mL graduated cup

1 metric ruler (optional)

For each student

1 Student Sheet 81.1, "Recording Results"

PROCEDURE

Part One: Collecting Evidence

1. If you have completed previous units of *Science and Life Issues*, review your notes from Activity 17, "Gas Exchange," and Activity 39, "Cells Alive!" Use your notes to complete Tables 1 and 2 on Student Sheet 81.1, "Recording Results." If you haven't completed these activities, your teacher will help you fill in the tables.

2. Fill a plastic cup half-full of water. (Your teacher may have already done this.) Add 15 drops of BTB.

3. Have one person in your group use a straw to blow into the BTB solution until it stops changing color. Record this as the initial BTB color in Table 3 of Student Sheet 81.1.

4. Place a piece of *Elodea* into one of the vials. Carefully fill the rest of this vial with your BTB solution. Cap the vial tightly and place it in the light.

5. Fill a second vial with the same BTB solution only. Cap this vial tightly and place alongside the first vial.

6. With your group, discuss what you think might happen. Record your prediction in your science notebook.

7. After at least 45 minutes (or during your next class period), observe your vials. Use your observations to complete Table 3 of Student Sheet 81.1, as well as Analysis Questions 1 and 2.

Part Two: The Role of Light

8. Design an experiment to investigate the role of light in plant photosynthesis. **Hint:** Use the introduction to the activity and your results from Part One to help you.

   When designing your experiment, think about the following questions:

   - What is the purpose of your experiment?
   - What variable are you testing?
   - What variables will you keep the same?
   - What is your hypothesis?
   - How many trials will you conduct?
   - Will you collect qualitative and/or quantitative data? How will these data help you to make a conclusion?
   - How will you record these data?

9. Record your hypothesis and your planned experimental procedure in your science notebook.

10. Make a data table that has space for all the data you need to record. You will fill it in during your experiment.

11. Obtain your teacher's approval of your experiment.

12. Conduct your experiment and record your results.

EXTENSION 1

Observe a capped vial containing a plant in BTB solution at different times of the day. What color is the solution first thing in the morning? At lunchtime? Explain your observations. What process may be taking place in plants at night?

ANALYSIS

Part One: Collecting Evidence

1. What was the purpose of the vial containing only BTB solution?

2. In the introduction to this activity, you were told that plants need carbon dioxide during photosynthesis. What evidence do you have from Part One of your investigation to support this claim?

Part Two: The Role of Light

3. Describe your experimental results. Use the word equation on page E-54 to help explain your results.

4. Explain the role that light plays in photosynthesis. How do your results provide evidence for your explanation?

5. A second-grader comes up to you and says, "We just learned that the sun made all the stuff in my lunch. But my lunch was a tuna sandwich." Using language a second-grader would understand, explain how the sun was the original source of the energy in the tuna sandwich. Then try out your explanation on a child you know!

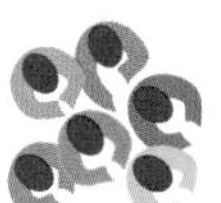

6. Think back to how the lake ecosystem described in Activity 79, "Eating for Energy," was affected by zebra mussels. Using your understanding of photosynthesis and ecosystems, explain why a decrease in phytoplankton allows more aquatic plants to grow on the lake bottom.

➢

EXTENSION 2

Your experiment looked at the *inputs* needed by a plant for photosynthesis. Design another experiment to collect evidence for the *outputs* of photosynthesis. Describe what materials you would need to perform this experiment, and what data you would collect.

82 The Cells of Producers

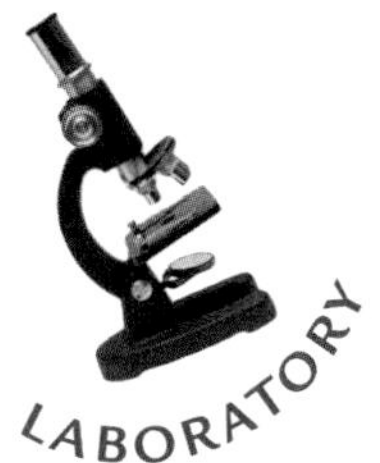

As you have been learning, producers such as plants play a unique role within an ecosystem. By transferring the sun's energy into chemical energy stored in food, plants provide energy in a form that can be used by consumers and decomposers. What is different about plants that allows them to do this? Find out by investigating the cells of plants and then comparing them to animal cells.

A botanist (a person who studies plants) gathers plants for his research.

CHALLENGE

How are the cells of producers such as plants different from the cells of consumers such as animals? How do plant cell structures relate to their function as producers?

➢

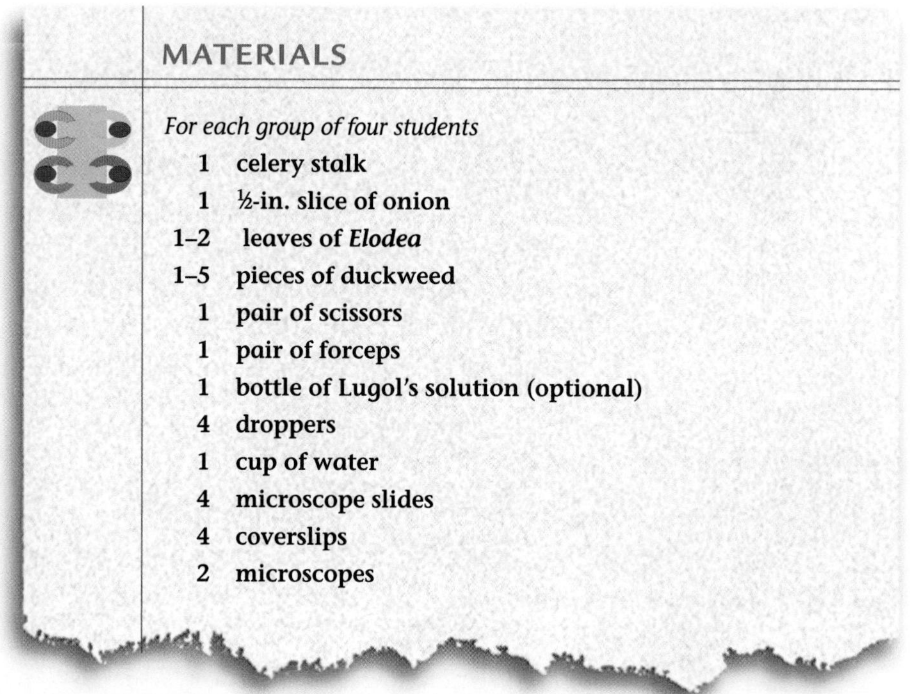

MATERIALS

For each group of four students

1 celery stalk
1 ½-in. slice of onion
1–2 leaves of *Elodea*
1–5 pieces of duckweed
1 pair of scissors
1 pair of forceps
1 bottle of Lugol's solution (optional)
4 droppers
1 cup of water
4 microscope slides
4 coverslips
2 microscopes

PROCEDURE

1. Have each person in your group complete one of the following four steps. You will share all four slides within your group.

   a. Pull a string of celery off the stalk. At the edge of the string, you will see a thin film. This is the outer layer of the celery stalk and the part where you will see plant cells most clearly. Use scissors to cut a short length of this outer film. Place this piece of celery on a microscope slide. Add a drop of water and slowly drop the coverslip, at an angle, into place (as shown in Figure 1).

   b. Get a small square of onion. Use your forceps to peel off a thin film of tissue from the inside layer of the onion square. Place this thin film on a microscope slide. Add a drop of water and slowly drop the coverslip, at an angle, into place (as shown in Figure 1).

   c. Get a piece of *Elodea* and break off a leaf. Place a piece of this leaf on a microscope slide. Add a drop of water and slowly drop the coverslip, at an angle, into place (as shown in Figure 1).

   d. Get a few leaves of duckweed. Place the leaves on a microscope slide. Add a drop of water and slowly drop the coverslip, at an angle, into place (as shown in Figure 1).

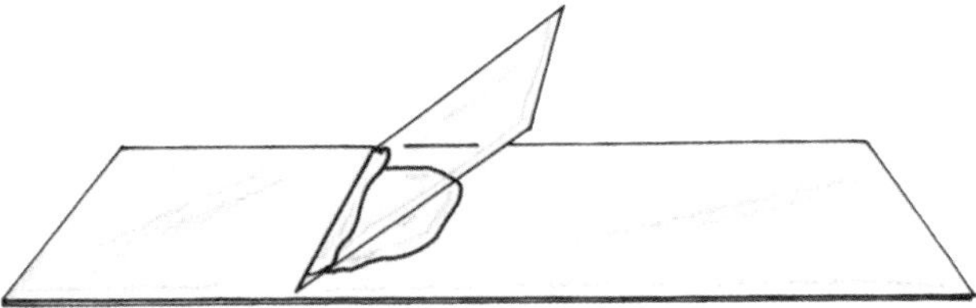

Figure 1: Placing the Coverslip

2. With your partner, observe the cells of each plant. Begin by observing the slide on low power (usually the 4x objective). Be sure that the plant material is in the center of the field of view (you may need to move the slide slightly) and completely in focus before going on to Step 3.

   Hint: When viewing celery, focus on the thinnest parts of the sample. When looking at duckweed, focus on the edges of the leaf.

3. Without moving the slide (which can be secured with stage clips), switch to medium power (usually the 10x objective). Adjust the microscope settings as necessary.

   Hint: If material on the slide is too dark to see, increase the amount of light on the slide: do this by slightly opening the diaphragm under the stage.

4. Turn the fine focus knob up and down just a little to reveal details of the plant cells at different levels of the slide.

5. Draw your observations of a cell from each plant. Be sure to record the type of plant and the level of magnification. Include details inside the cell and along the edge of the cell membrane on your drawing.

6. Look again at the duckweed, but this time look at a root. Draw your observations of the cells that you see in the duckweed root.

7. When you have completed your observations, turn off the microscope light and set the microscope back to low power.

EXTENSION

Place a drop of salt water at the edge of the coverslip while looking at *Elodea*. What happens? What does this tell you about the importance of fresh water to plants?

➢

ANALYSIS

1. Using various microscope techniques, scientists have identified the structures most commonly found in plant cells. Some of these structures are shown in the diagram of the plant cell shown in Figure 2. Not all plant cells contain every structure, though most plant cells do contain the majority of them. However, some of these structures are very difficult to observe if you only use a light microscope.

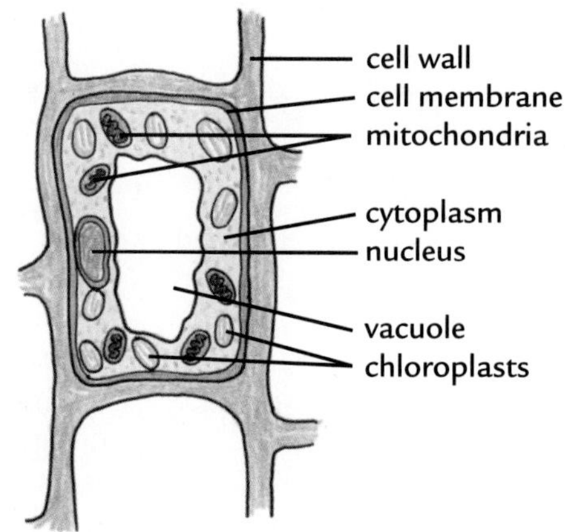

Figure 2: A Plant Cell

   a. Which cell structures appear to be ones that you observed? List them.

   b. Which cell structures were not visible to you? List them.

2. Compare the various plant cells you observed. Which cell structures did all of the plant cells appear to have in common?

3. Look at the simplified diagram of an animal cell shown in Figure 3. Animal cells, as well as plant cells, contain many structures; this diagram shows only some of these structures.

   a. Which cell—plant or animal—is the cell of a consumer?

   b. Compare the plant cell diagram with the animal cell diagram. Based on these diagrams, what structures would you expect to find in both plant and animal cells?

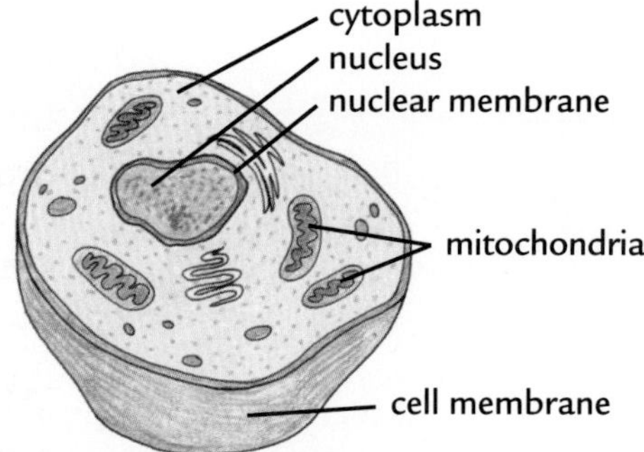

Figure 3: An Animal Cell

   c. Based on your comparisons, which structure(s) within a plant cell do you think is most important in food production?

4. Copy a larger version of the Venn diagram shown here. Complete it by writing in the characteristics of animal cells, plant cells, and bacterial cells (which you may have first studied in Activity 44, "Who's Who?"). Record unique features of each type of cell in the individual spaces. Record common features among groups in the spaces that overlap.

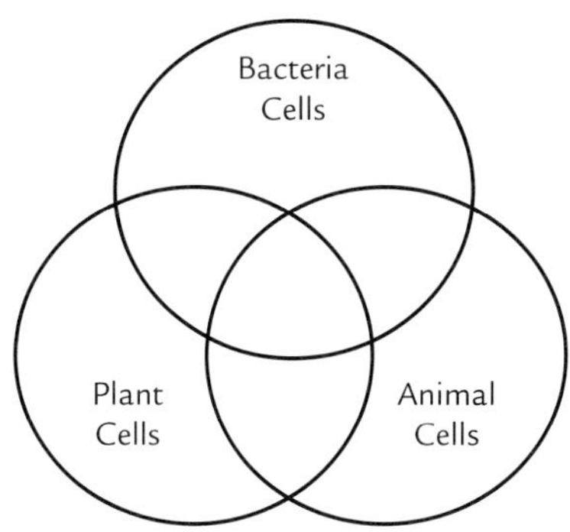

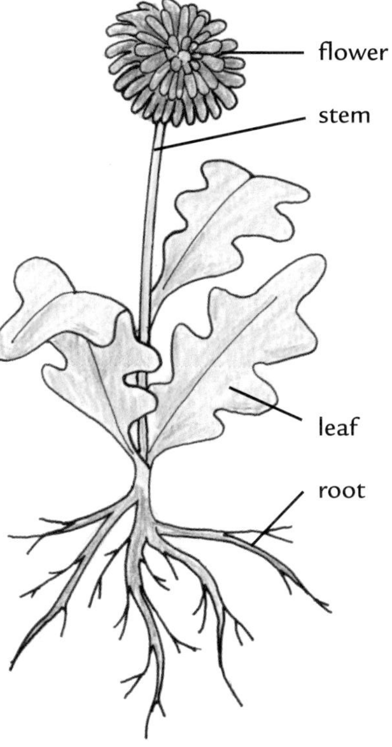

5. a. Many plants have leaves, stems, roots, and—during the blooming season—flowers. Which of these parts are likely to absorb sunlight and carry out photosynthesis?

   b. Of the cells you observed—celery stem, onion, *Elodea* leaf, duckweed leaf, and duckweed root—which would you expect to carry out photosynthesis?

   c. What cell structures are seen only in cells that absorb sunlight and carry out photosynthesis?

6. Three of the introduced species described in Activity 73, "Introduced Species," are plants: kudzu, purple loosestrife, and hydrilla. Each of these plants is growing successfully in different parts of the United States, partly because they are very well adapted to absorb sunlight and carry out photosynthesis.

   a. What effect do you think the growth and spread of these introduced plants will have on native plants? Explain.

   b. What effect do you think the growth and spread of these introduced plants will have on animals in the native ecosystems? Explain.

83 A Suitable Habitat

Introduced species do not always survive in new environments. This is because all species have requirements for the place in which they can live. These requirements define the species' **habitat** (HAB-ih-tat). What makes up a habitat? Think about different aquatic ecosystems, such as a small pond or a coral reef. While both of these environments contain water, they have very different characteristics. Coral reefs are found in the ocean, which contains salt water, while most ponds are freshwater. An organism that lives in freshwater, like a zebra mussel, cannot survive in the coral reef environment. The photos below show several different habitats.

Producers, consumers, and decomposers are the living components of an ecosystem. Every ecosystem also has many non-living elements, such as rainfall, light, and temperature. The interaction of all these determines whether a habitat is suitable for a specific organism.

CHALLENGE

What are some of the important non-living characteristics of a habitat?

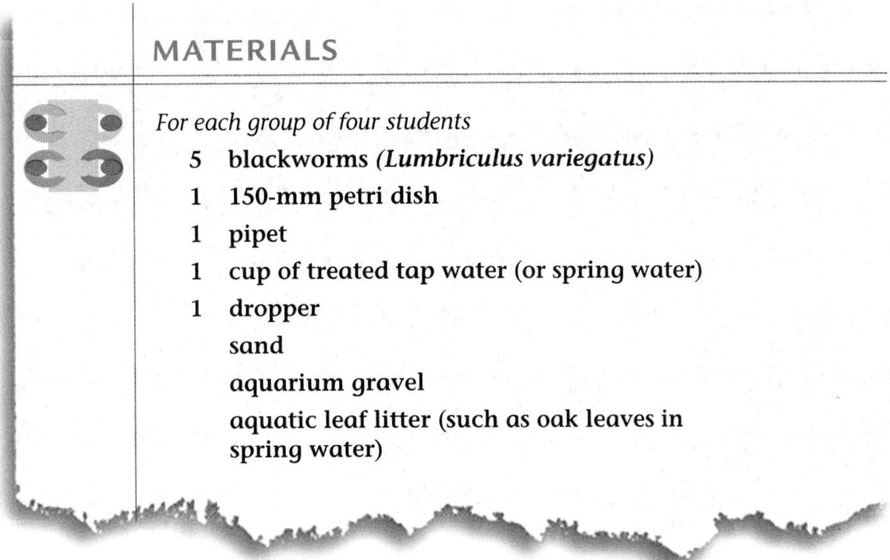

MATERIALS

For each group of four students

- 5 **blackworms *(Lumbriculus variegatus)***
- 1 **150-mm petri dish**
- 1 **pipet**
- 1 **cup of treated tap water (or spring water)**
- 1 **dropper**
- **sand**
- **aquarium gravel**
- **aquatic leaf litter (such as oak leaves in spring water)**

PROCEDURE

1. Fill the base of a petri dish with treated tap water (or spring water) and place 5 blackworms in it.
2. Observe how the blackworms respond over the next few minutes. Discuss with your group any behaviors that seem to be true of all or most of the blackworms.
3. As a class, discuss what type of data you could collect on the blackworms in order to determine which type(s) of material provides a good habitat for them.
4. Compare the different materials you can use to create a blackworm habitat. Record any similarities and differences in the physical characteristics of the different habitat materials.

➢

5. With your group, design an experiment to investigate which type(s) of material provides a good blackworm habitat.

   When designing your experiment, think about the following questions:

   - What is the purpose of your experiment?
   - What variable are you testing?
   - What variables will you keep the same?
   - What is your hypothesis?
   - How many trials will you conduct?
   - Will you collect qualitative and/or quantitative data? How will these data help you to make a conclusion?
   - How will you record these data?

6. Record your hypothesis and your planned experimental procedure in your science notebook.

7. Make a data table that has space for all the data you need to record. You will fill it in during your experiment.

8. Obtain your teacher's approval of your experiment.

9. Conduct your experiment and record your results.

ANALYSIS

1. Based on your experiment, which type(s) of material provides a good habitat for blackworms? Explain how your experimental results support your conclusions.

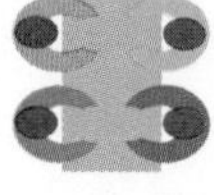

2. Describe the non-living characteristics of a habitat. **Hint:** What non-living factors could affect whether organisms will survive and reproduce?

3. What could you do with your blackworms to investigate if a warm or cold habitat is better for them? Write a procedure that anyone in your class could follow to investigate this question.

4. **Reflection:** Do you think that introduced species are always successful in new environments? Explain.

Clam Catch

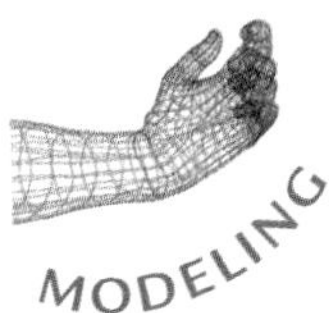

Populations usually vary from season to season and year to year, often depending on non-living factors such as rainfall or temperature variations. Populations of a species can also be affected by living factors, such as other species that may provide food, compete for food, or provide shade or shelter.

When a new species is introduced into an area, it can compete with native species for food and other resources. Clams and zebra mussels are both mollusks that feed by filtering plankton from the water. What happens when zebra mussels are introduced into a habitat containing a clam population?

Zebra mussels growing on a native clam

How might the introduction of a competing species, such as zebra mussels, affect a population of native clams?

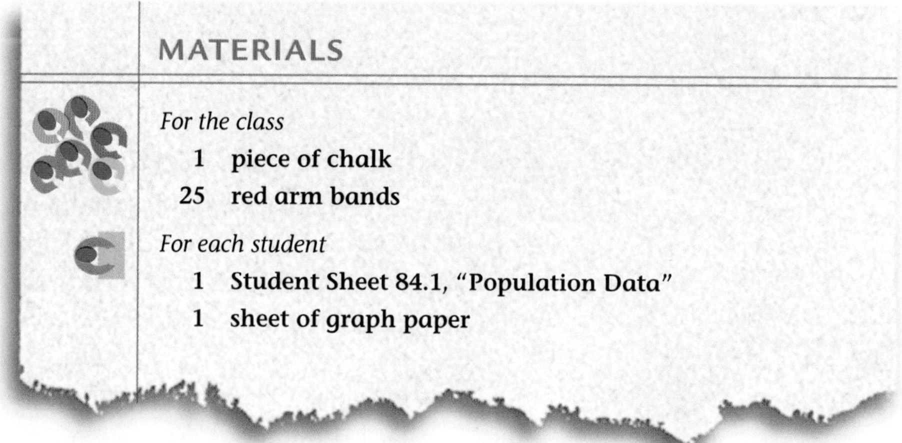

PROCEDURE

Part One: Clam Population Size

1. As directed by your teacher, determine which students will initially represent clams and which students will initially represent plankton.
2. If you represent a clam, stand inside a chalk circle. There should be only one clam per circle. The space between the clams represents the amount of space a clam needs to survive. As long as you represent a clam, you must stay inside the circle.
3. If you represent plankton, stand behind the safety line on one side of the clam bed.
4. Your teacher will instruct the plankton to run through the clam bed, from one safety zone to the other (see Figure 1). A clam can use only one hand to tag its food. Each clam will try to "catch" (tag) plankton to survive; any plankton that is caught becomes a clam and has to find a home circle. Any clam that does not catch any plankton dies from lack of food; the student becomes plankton and must go to the safety zone.
5. Count and record the total population of clams.
6. Repeat Steps 4 and 5 at least ten times.

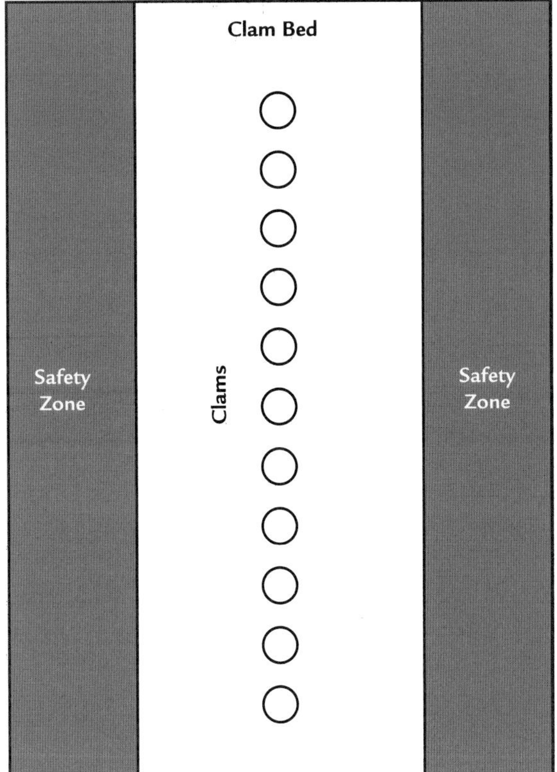

Figure 1: Map of Clam Catch Game

Part Two: Competition

7. Zebra mussels have invaded the clam bed! As directed by your teacher, determine which students will initially represent clams, which students will initially represent plankton, and which students will initially represent zebra mussels.

8. If you represent a zebra mussel, wear an arm band to identify yourself and then stand inside a chalk circle. Since zebra mussels grow very close together, a zebra mussel can grow in (i.e. share) the same circle as a clam. If no clams are present, two zebra mussels can occupy the same circle. As long as you represent a zebra mussel, you must stay inside a circle.

9. If you represent a clam, stand inside a chalk circle. There can still be only one clam per circle (although one zebra mussel can occupy the same circle). As long as you represent a clam, you must stay inside the circle.

10. If you represent plankton, stand behind the safety line on one side of the clam bed.

11. Your teacher will instruct the plankton to run through the clam bed, from one safety zone to the other (see Figure 1). A clam can use only one hand to tag its food, while a zebra mussel can use both hands. Each clam and zebra mussel will try to catch plankton to survive; any plankton that is caught becomes a clam or a zebra mussel (depending on who catches it). If you become a zebra mussel, collect an arm band to wear.

    Any clam or zebra mussel that does not catch any plankton dies from lack of food and becomes plankton. When a zebra mussel dies, the arm band should be removed.

12. Record and count the total population of clams and zebra mussels.

13. Repeat Steps 11 and 12 at least ten times.

14. Record the class data on Student Sheet 88.1, "Population Data."

EXTENSION

Are Introduced Species Always Successful?

Introduce a mobile predator that eats only clams. Figure out how to modify the game to include this predator. Predict what you think will happen to the predator population and the clam population over time. Then test your ideas by playing the game for at least ten rounds.

ANALYSIS

Part One: Clam Population

1. a. Graph the population of clams over time from Part One of the Procedure. Decide which type of graph (bar or line) would best represent the data. Remember to label your axes and to title your graph.

   b. Look at your graph and describe how this population of clams changed over time.

2. What factor limited the size of the clam population?

Part Two: Competition

3. a. Graph the population of clams and zebra mussels over time from Part Two of the Procedure. Use the same type of graph you used in Part One. Remember to label your axes and to title your graph. Use a key to show what represents the clam population and what represents the zebra mussel population.

   b. Look at your graph and describe how the population of clams changed over time.

   c. Look at your graph and describe how the population of zebra mussels changed over time.

4. a. What happened to the clam population after zebra mussels were introduced?

   b. Why did zebra mussels have this effect on the clam population? Explain.

5. a. In a real lake, what non-living factors might affect the size of clam and zebra mussel populations? List them. **Hint:** Go outside and look at an ecosystem around you. Observing an actual ecosystem may help you think of more factors.

   b. In a real lake, what living factors might affect the size of clam and zebra mussel populations? List them.

85 Is There Room for One More?

In this unit, you've learned to interpret population graphs and to analyze effects of factors such as competition, predators, and various environmental conditions on population size. Can a population graph tell you how much room there is for a particular species in a habitat? What does it mean for a population to run out of space?

What is carrying capacity?

READING

Imagine that you are a field ecologist. You've been studying a small lake called Lake Ness for the past ten years. You first began work at the lake when you heard that zebra mussels had invaded a nearby river, one that connects to Lake Ness. After ten years of study, you feel satisfied that you have a good idea of how quickly the zebra mussel can populate a lake of this size. You've been keeping an ongoing count of the zebra mussels in the lake (in mussels per square meter). At this point, your graph of population size looks like Graph 1.

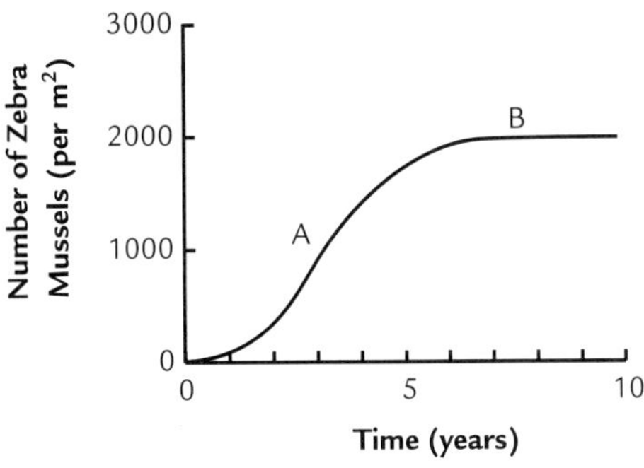

Graph 1: Zebra Mussel Population of Lake Ness Over 10 Years

STOPPING TO THINK 1

Recall that zebra mussels get their food by filtering plankton out of the water. Look at Graph 1. What do you think is happening to the quantity of plankton at:

a. Point A? Explain your reasoning.

b. Point B? Explain your reasoning.

As a result of your analysis, you think you have identified the maximum number of zebra mussels that could live successfully in Lake Ness. You think this might be the **carrying capacity** of the lake for zebra mussels. This term suggests the amount a container can hold, or carry. But unlike the capacity of a container, the number of zebra mussels that the lake can successfully hold may change over time, based on both living and non-living factors.

A few days later, your friend Nadia comes to visit you from the city. She drove up to the lake in her new car. "It has a carrying capacity of five passengers," she brags. Since you've never seen her drive anyone but her best friend and her dog, you simply shrug.

STOPPING TO THINK 2

a. Look again at Graph 1. What is the carrying capacity of zebra mussels in Lake Ness? How did you determine this?

b. List some of the factors that might affect this carrying capacity.

After Nadia leaves, you spend a week organizing your data. You decide to stop studying Lake Ness so closely for a while. Instead, you decide you'll return once a year to camp at the lake. During each visit, you can check on the zebra mussel population. Fifteen years pass. A graph of your data now looks like Graph 2.

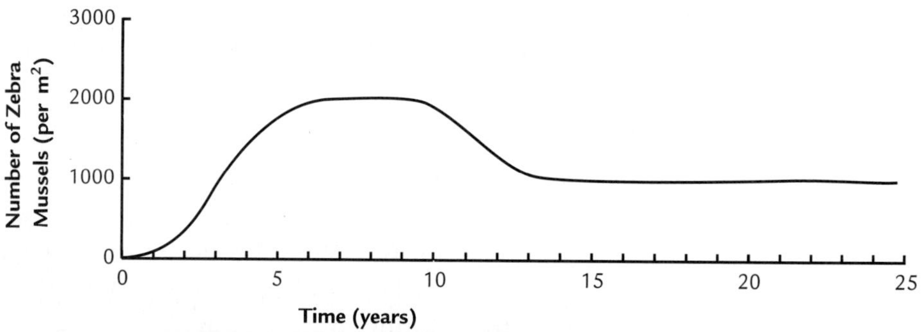

Graph 2: Zebra Mussel Population of Lake Ness Over 25 Years

STOPPING TO THINK 3

a. What is the carrying capacity for zebra mussels in Lake Ness between Years 13 and 25?

b. Identify at least three non-living factors that may have caused the carrying capacity to change. Explain how each factor could cause this change in carrying capacity.

c. Identify at least three living factors that may have caused the carrying capacity to change. Explain how each factor could cause this change in carrying capacity.

d. Do you think that the zebra mussel population will return to the level it had reached between Years 5 and 10? Why or why not?

For twelve years now, you've been puzzled by the change in the zebra mussel population. For example, in all your years of study, you've found no evidence of a new predator of zebra mussels appearing in the lake. You remain convinced that something about the zebra mussel's habitat must have changed to cause this shift in the population level. Consulting public records, you discover that a new factory was built just three miles from the lake about fifteen years ago!

Energized, you decide to test your hypothesis. You set up two identical tanks. One tank contains water from Lake Ness. The other tank contains water from a similar lake that is higher up in the mountains and farther from the factory. You add exactly ten adult zebra mussels to each tank. Every day, you supply the two tanks with fresh plankton, which you culture in a separate tank. Several months later, you are puzzled to find no difference at all in the zebra mussel populations of the two tanks.

STOPPING TO THINK 4

Is this a good experiment to test the hypothesis that the factory was affecting the zebra mussel population? Explain.

➢

ANALYSIS

1. Shown below is the population graph from the Analysis section of Activity 78, "Coughing Up Clues."

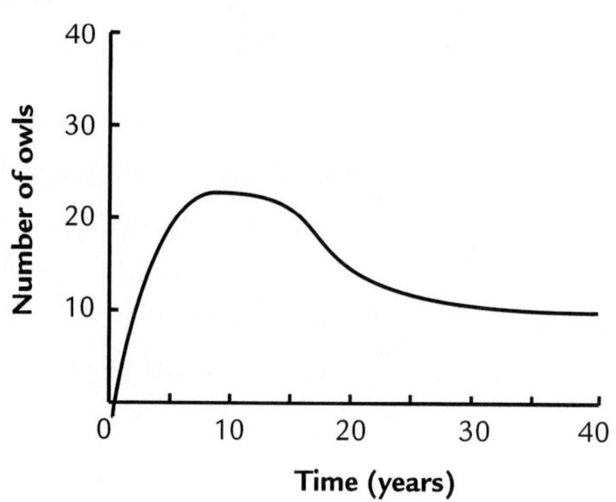

   a. What is the carrying capacity for owls in this habitat?

   b. How did the carrying capacity change during this 40-year period? Explain.

   c. What living and non-living factors might explain this change in carrying capacity?

2. Turn back to Activity 72, "The Miracle Fish?" and look at Figure 2. Can you determine the carrying capacity of Nile perch in Lake Victoria based on this graph? Explain.

3. **Reflection:** Consider the introduced species you have been researching. Identify one ecosystem into which it has been introduced. Do you think this species has reached its carrying capacity in this ecosystem? Explain.

86 Taking a Look Outside

Until now, you have focused on studying ecology in the laboratory. But ecology is the study of living organisms in the physical environment. This means that a majority of ecological study is done in the natural habitat of organisms, which is usually outdoors. This type of outdoor investigation is known as **field study.** The scientist you read about in Activity 85, "Is There Room for One More?" performed a long-term field study of Lake Ness.

The "field" in field study can refer to any kind of ecosystem.

What do you observe when you conduct a field study?

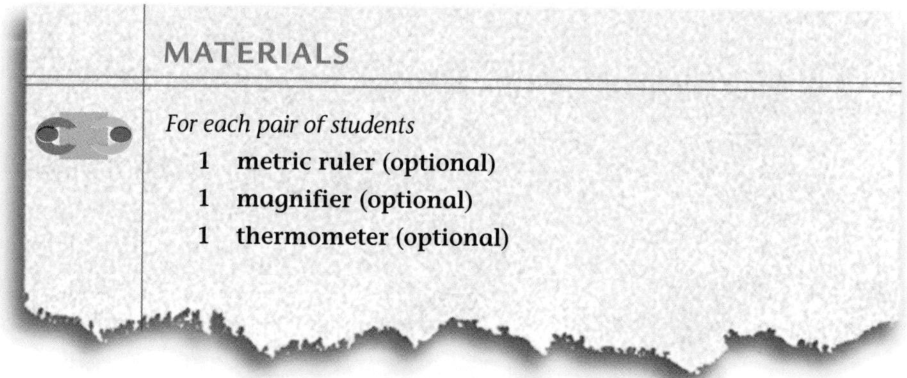

PROCEDURE

1. Select an ecosystem on your school grounds or near your school. Think about locations where you are most likely to observe interactions between living and non-living factors. Be sure to consider all of the possible habitats that are available in the area. For example, an overhanging roof may be home to a population of birds. Long grasses may contain many small animals, such as insects. Streams or ponds are also excellent places for field study.
2. Spend some time carefully observing your ecosystem. Start by simply sitting quietly and watching. Then record all the different types of habitat found within your ecosystem. For example, if you chose a small pond, you might identify the pond edge, the shallow water, and the deep water as three different types of habitat.
3. Record the characteristics of each habitat found within your ecosystem. For example, how much light and oxygen are available? How much rainfall is your habitat likely to receive? What is the temperature within the habitat? Will the temperature change a lot over a 24-hour period? Over the entire year?
4. Look for the presence of living organisms within your ecosystem. You may observe living creatures by gently looking among the different habitats, such as under leaves and rocks, or you may observe signs, such as animal tracks or other disturbances, that show that living creatures have been through the habitat.

5. Study your habitat for the next few days:

   a. Every day, observe your ecosystem for at least five minutes. Note any changes that occur. You may want to consider making your observations as an answer to a question, such as "Do I observe more species in the shady part of this ecosystem compared to the sunlit areas?"

   b. Quantitatively investigate one physical factor, such as temperature. Do this by taking measurements of this factor each time you observe your ecosystem.

6. If possible, create a food web for the organisms within your ecosystem. Identify the role (producer, consumer, or decomposer) that each organism plays within the ecosystem.

ANALYSIS

1. Summarize the results of your field study. What did you learn about this ecosystem? How did the physical factor you measured change over time? Was there any relationship between your observations and the physical factor you measured?

2. Compare the advantages of field study vs. laboratory work in studying ecology. Explain your ideas.

3. You may have seen documentaries or read books on ecosystems around the world. How do you think the information presented in these sources is gathered?

4. Many ecologists spend their entire lives studying a single ecosystem or population of organisms. For example, Dian Fossey spent almost 19 years studying the mountain gorillas of central Africa. Jane Goodall spent many years studying chimpanzees in their natural environment. Today, ecologists study ecosystems and organisms in all different parts of the world. Why do you think people spend their lives studying such systems? What can such studies tell us about the natural environment?

5. **Reflection:** How did field study differ from your laboratory work on ecology?

87 Too Many Mussels?

Having completed his research project, Ondar has a dilemma. He wants to do something about the problem of introduced species. He's particularly concerned about zebra mussels, which have been found in rivers and lakes around his state. What, if anything, should he do?

What are the trade-offs of trying to control an introduced species?

In this photo, you can see zebra mussel shells piled along the beach in a stack more than a foot high.

PROCEDURE

Read the statements of each of the following people. Decide what you would do if you were Ondar.

Johnson Poole, Engineer, Mantee Water Treatment Plant

"Zebra mussels cause a lot of problems for us. We supply water to the city of Mantee. It's our job to provide clean water for homes and businesses. To do that, large pipes bring water into the plant from Bear Lake. Here at the plant, we filter and treat the water before sending it on to the city.

"But we've had a hard time lately getting the water into the plant. Those zebra mussels grow on everything, including the insides of the pipes. We have seen up to 750,000 zebra mussels in a square meter of pipe! As you might imagine, all of these zebra mussels begin to block the flow of water.

A worker uses a hose to suction zebra mussels from inside a pipe at a power plant.

"Right now, we shut down the plant every few months. Then we send someone into the pipes to physically remove all the mussels. This costs tons of money—the U.S. Fish and Wildlife Service reports that dealing with this problem in the Great Lakes area alone has cost billions of dollars!

"In the meantime, we're looking at other solutions. For instance, we're exploring ways to prevent zebra mussels from settling and growing on the pipes in the first place. Zebra mussels grow best on hard surfaces, such as rocks. That's also why they sometimes grow on other animals with hard shells like clams. We're trying to find out if we can coat the pipes with some type of paint or something else that would prevent the mussels from growing on them. You could say we're trying to make the pipes a less suitable habitat for the mussels!"

➢

Adrienne Vogel, Chemist, Bear Industrial Company

"Our company uses water from Bear Lake. Chemicals have been shown to kill both larval and adult zebra mussels. That's one way we prevent zebra mussels from growing in our water supply. We can't afford for zebra mussels to grow inside our water containment ponds. So, after the water comes into our plant, we treat it with a variety of chemicals. While this is very effective in dealing with the zebra mussels, the treated water does contain a lot of chemicals. This means that we can't release the water back into the lake as is. Luckily for us, we are able to recycle and re-use the water within the company for several months. Before we release the water, we treat it to isolate the chemicals and dispose of them according to state regulations. But this all costs money."

Talia Mercata, Biologist, State Fish and Wildlife Service

"I sympathize with the people at both plants. Humans are not the only ones that are affected by zebra mussels. Zebra mussels may be changing the native ecology of lakes and rivers. We know that Bear Lake is clearer as a result of zebra mussels. Some people think this is a good thing. One thing is certain—zebra mussels have filtered out so much of the algae that they may be changing the feeding structure of the lake.

"Some scientists are investigating how predators may help control zebra mussel populations. In Europe, where zebra mussels first came from, there are a lot more native predators, such as fish that have teeth. Here in the U.S., the populations of fish that might be good predators aren't that high.

"Ducks are one possible predator here in the U.S. But using predators to control zebra mussels is complicated. How do you control where ducks and fish decide to search for food? How can you guarantee that they'll eat zebra mussels and not some other food? How will they reduce populations in hard-to-reach areas, such as inside pipes? What happens if the introduction of the predator causes other imbalances in the ecosystem?

"Because of these difficulties, my research focuses on the use of parasites to control zebra mussels. If my research is successful, I may identify a parasite that could infect and kill zebra mussels. I'm not sure how quickly this would affect their populations, though."

Henry Wai, Activist, People for Responsible Action

"It's a shame that zebra mussels were ever introduced into the United States. We can only predict how they'll affect the ecology of our lakes and rivers. We don't know for sure.

This outboard motor is covered with zebra mussels.

"People caused this problem in the first place and I think every person should take responsibility for trying to prevent further damage. It's easy to forget that things we do every day might contribute to the problem of introduced species, but it's true.

"For example, just carrying equipment like inner tubes and diving gear from one lake to another can introduce a species like the zebra mussel. After all, its larval stage is very small. That's why it's important for people to rinse and dry their equipment before going from one body of water to another. Think about it—if every boater, fisher, swimmer, and diver took care to clean off his or her equipment, we might prevent zebra mussels and other organisms from spreading across the U.S. so quickly!"

EXTENSION

Go to the SALI page of the SEPUP website for links to sites with information about zebra mussels and management options.

ANALYSIS

1. What, if anything, do you think should be done about the growing population of zebra mussels in the United States? Support your answer with evidence and discuss the trade-offs of your decision.

   Hint: To write a complete answer, first state your opinion. Provide two or more pieces of evidence that support your opinion. Then discuss the trade-offs of your decision.

88 Presenting the Facts

Introduced species can have an enormous impact on the economy as well as on native ecosystems. Your research project and your study of ecology have helped you to become an expert on one introduced species. Why are some introduced species more likely to be successful than others?

What, if anything, should be done about the introduction of a new species into an ecosystem?

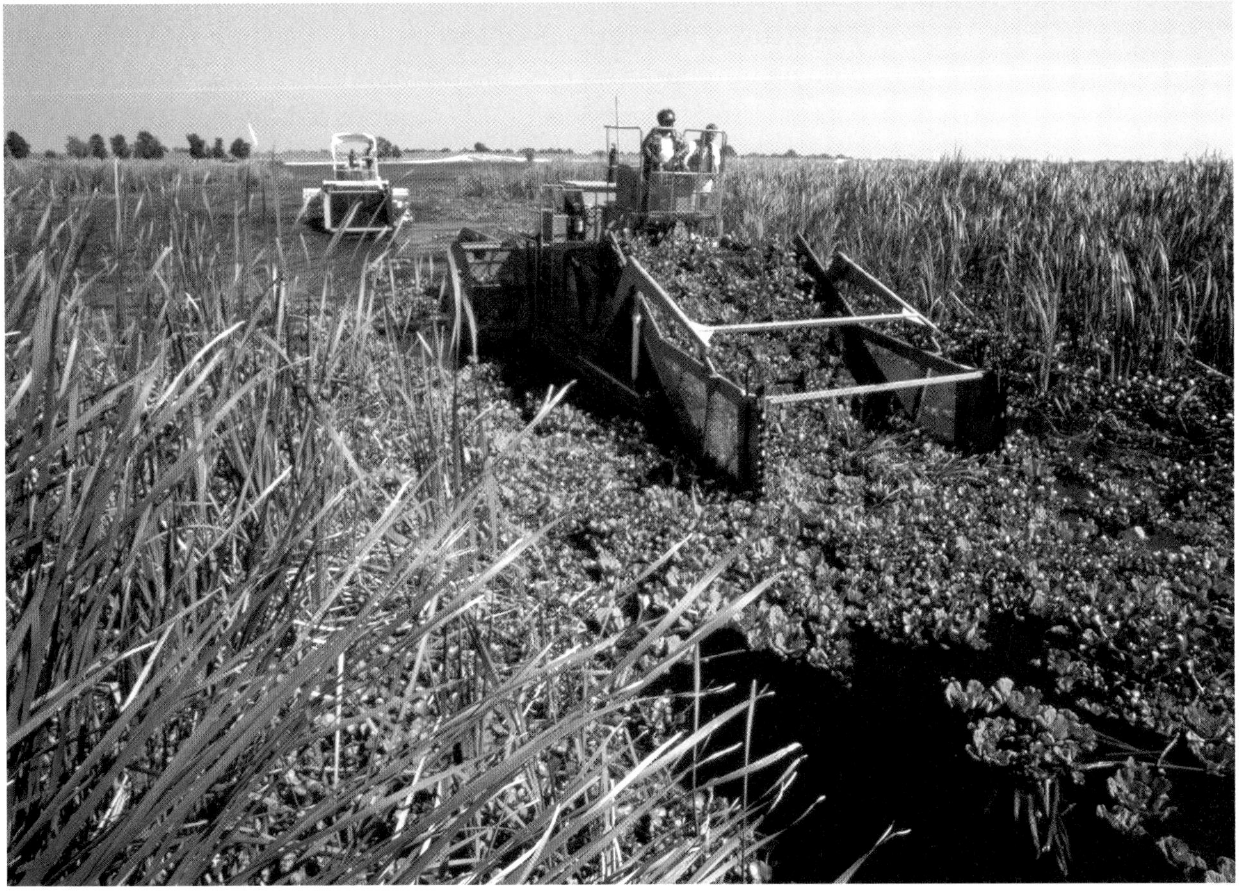

These workers are removing hydrilla and other aquatic plants from a lake.

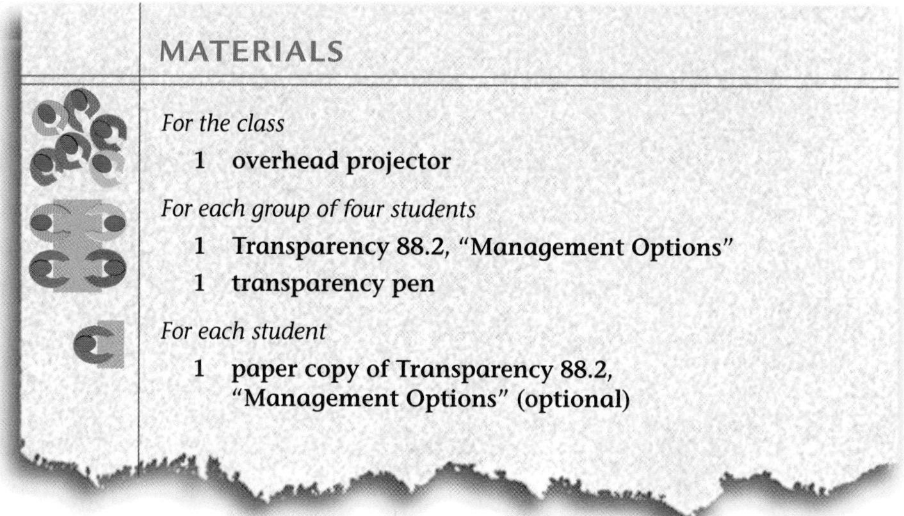

PROCEDURE

1. In Activity 73, "Introduced Species," you began a research project on an introduced species. You will now present your research to the class. Use Student Sheet 73.1, "Introduced Species Research," as you plan your presentation. Your presentation should help your audience make an informed decision about what, if anything, to do about this introduced species.

   When planning your presentation, remember:

   - All the members of your group must participate.
   - Since any group member may be asked to answer questions from the class, all group members should fully understand the report.
   - Your presentation time is limited.
   - Many people learn best from a mix of visual, written, and spoken information. Include graphs and maps when possible.
   - While you have your own opinions on this issue, it is important that you present unbiased and complete information. The members of your audience can then make their own decisions.
   - You may want to role-play different experts when presenting your information, such as the people who might present information at a city council meeting. The class would represent the community members who would be voting on a decision.

2. List all of the options that are available for dealing with your introduced species on Transparency 88.2, "Management Options."
3. Begin by presenting general information about your introduced species to the class. Respond to any questions that other students may have.
4. Ask the class what they think are the pros and cons of each of the options you presented. Record their responses on Transparency 88.2.
5. If you are aware of issues that were not brought up by the class, add them onto the transparency.
6. Have the class vote on what, if anything, should be done about the introduction of this species into new ecosystems.
7. Listen to and participate in other groups' presentations.

ANALYSIS

1. Many species are accidentally introduced into North American ecosystems from other countries each year. The opposite is also true: North American species are also introduced into other countries.
   a. What other countries or other areas of the United States are most likely to exchange species with the area where you live?
   b. Only a small fraction of species that are introduced are successful enough to create problems in their new environment. What features of a species do you think make it likely to be successful in a new environment? Use specific examples from the project presentations in your answer.
2. How do you think the number of introduced species in the United States will change over the next 50 years? Explain your reasoning.
3. Write a letter to the editor of a local newspaper describing the situation of an introduced species. Explain what, if anything, you think should be done about the species. Support your answer with evidence and discuss the trade-offs of your decision.

   Hint: To write a complete answer, first state your opinion. Provide two or more pieces of evidence that support your opinion. Then discuss the trade-offs of your decision.

Evolution

F

Unit F

Evolution

It was Kenya's fourth visit to the pet store. Ever since she decided she wanted a pet lizard for her birthday, she had tried to come every day. She still hadn't decided which lizard she would like to have—and her birthday was less than a week away!

"Excuse me, young lady, can I help you?" asked the sales clerk behind the counter.

"I want a lizard for my birthday," replied Kenya. "But I can't decide which one I like best. There are so many different kinds—and they look so different."

"Some of them eat different foods, too," added the sales clerk.

"I don't understand how there can be so many different kinds of the same animal," said Kenya. "It's amazing! I wonder how it happened."

• • •

Have you ever wondered about the amazing variety of organisms on Earth? How did they evolve? How are they related? Just as historians study the history of humans, some scientists study the history of life on Earth. They do this by gathering evidence, making connections, creating models, and testing theories. In this unit, you will learn to interpret the many sources of evidence that exist for the evolution of life on Earth.

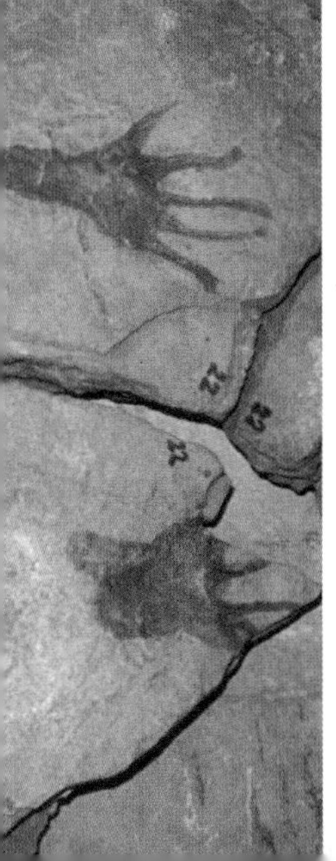

89 Here Today, Gone Tomorrow?

When the last member of a species dies without any surviving offspring, we say that that species has become **extinct**. Every species alive today is related to many other species that have already become extinct. Becoming extinct is not a sign of inferiority, but just another sign that ecosystems are constantly changing. In fact, it is estimated that 99.9% of all species that have ever lived on Earth are now extinct. Today, species that have such a small population that they are in danger of becoming extinct are called **endangered species**.

What are the trade-offs in deciding whether to save an endangered species or to re-create an extinct one?

Extinct animals include dinosaurs and saber-toothed cats.

Endangered animals include tigers and gorillas.

PROCEDURE

Work with your group to read and discuss the story of mammoths and modern elephants.

Mammoths and Elephants

You may know that dinosaurs became extinct about 65 million years ago, 64 million years before humans evolved. There is evidence that at least one enormous asteroid crashed into Earth at that time. Many scientists believe that this created huge clouds of dust that blocked out the sun for a long period of time. As you learned in the Ecology unit, producers form the base of the food web. A loss of sunlight would cause the death of many producer species, which, in turn, would cause the death of many consumer species, such as dinosaurs. By the time the dust settled and sunlight could reach Earth's surface, thousands of species, including the dinosaurs, had become extinct and most ecosystems were greatly changed.

One species that became extinct much more recently is the mammoth. If mammoths were still around, they would be close relatives of the elephants living on Earth today. The entire bodies of some mammoths were trapped during the most recent ice age and have remained frozen ever since. Explorers have tasted mammoth meat, as have several curious scientists! Some scientists think that the tissue of frozen mammoths is in good enough shape to bring mammoths back from the dead.

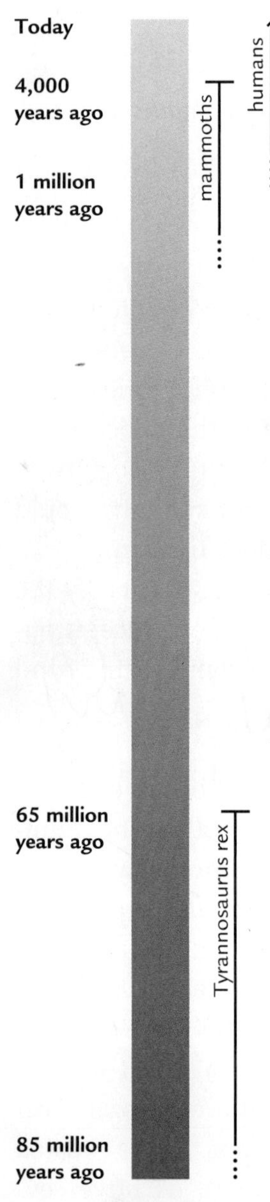

Figure 1: Timeline

Mammoths evolved 3 to 4 million years ago, about 60 million years after dinosaurs became extinct (Figure 1). Mammoths thrived and spread to North America about 1.8 million years ago. But about 10,000 years ago, all but a few small herds of mammoths died. The last mammoth died around 4,000 years ago. There is no evidence that an asteroid or other catastrophic event brought about the extinction of the mammoths.

What did happen 10,000 years ago that caused this huge drop in the mammoth population? One possibility is that the mammoths could not survive the drastic changes in climate and vegetation that occurred when the last ice age ended. In addition, humans—who lived at the same time as the mammoths—were moving into new environments as their population grew. The end of the last ice age helped expand the range of humans into areas where mammoths lived. Increased hunting of mammoths by humans may have contributed to their extinction.

While mammoths and modern elephants are closely related, mammoths are not direct ancestors of modern elephants. In fact, until the mammoth became extinct, mammoths and elephants were alive in different parts of the world. Based on fossil remains, the common ancestor of both modern elephants and mammoths is estimated to have lived 4 to 5 million years ago. The fossil considered to be the first member of their order is dated at about 55 million years ago. Since then, scientists believe that there have been over 500 different elephant and mammoth species. Only two of these species are alive today: the Asian (or Indian) elephant and the African elephant. Figure 2 shows a "family tree" including modern elephants and several extinct relatives. Populations of both African and Asian elephants are declining, and the Asian elephant is considered an endangered species.

The Asian elephant is smaller than the African, with smaller ears and a slightly rounded or flat back. Asian elephants have a double-domed forehead (African elephants have only a single dome). In addition, Asian elephants have a single "finger" on the upper tip of the trunk, while African elephants have a second on the lower tip.

African elephant

Asian elephant

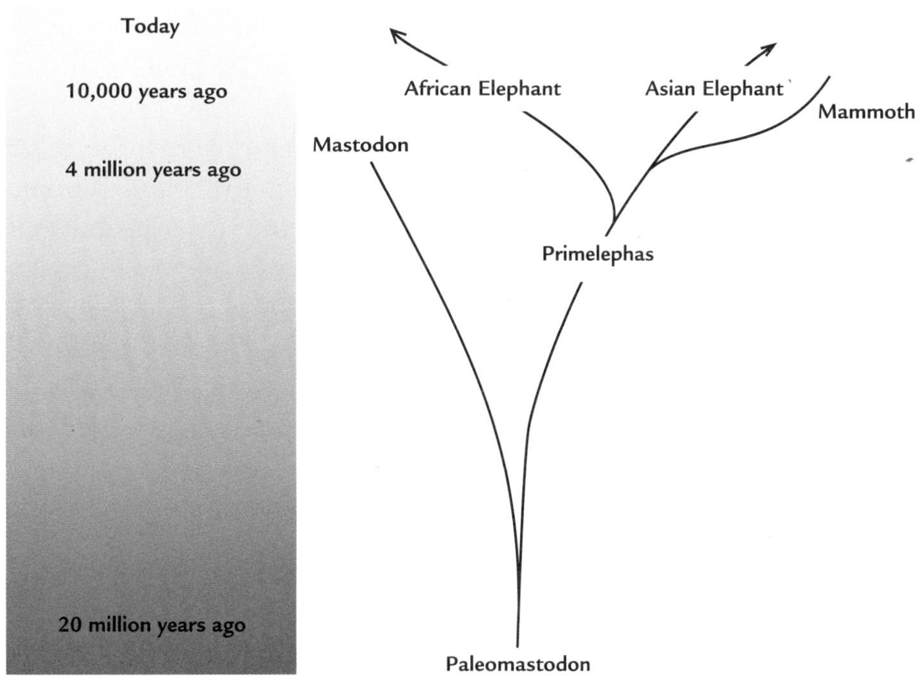

Figure 2: Evolution of Modern Elephants

Unlike African elephants, which all have tusks, only the male Asian elephants have them. In fact, even some of the male Asian elephants do not grow tusks! Killing elephants for their ivory is illegal in India and China. Still, most of the large-tusked male Asian elephants have already been killed for their ivory.

Asian elephants used to roam from Iran to southern Asia (Figure 3). In the early 1900s, approximately 250,000 Asian elephants lived in the wild. Today, it is estimated that no more than 50,000 Asian elephants are left. Their population has declined by more than 80% in less than 100 years! Without intervention, Asian elephants will most likely become extinct. By passing laws, raising money, creating wildlife preserves, and raising awareness, some people are working hard to save the Asian elephant.

Not all people are fighting to save Asian elephants. Asian elephants are forest animals. As the human population increases, forests have been cut down to build farms and villages. Today, most wild Asian elephants have been forced to live in hill and mountain regions. A single adult elephant eats about 330 pounds of grasses, roots, leaves, and bark each day, and these environments cannot always supply enough food. Elephant herds often seek out nearby farms that grow crops such as sugar cane and grains. These farms suffer crop loss, property damage, and even loss of life. In an average year, Asian elephants kill approximately 300 people in India alone.

Loss of habitat, combined with human hunting, has caused the decline in the Asian elephant population, a situation similar to that faced by the mammoth several thousand years ago. Should the Asian elephant be saved, or should this species be allowed to become extinct, just like the mammoth and millions of other species before it? Are people spending too much time, energy, and money trying to save endangered species? Or should efforts be increased, perhaps by going so far as to try to re-create extinct species, as has been proposed for the mammoth?

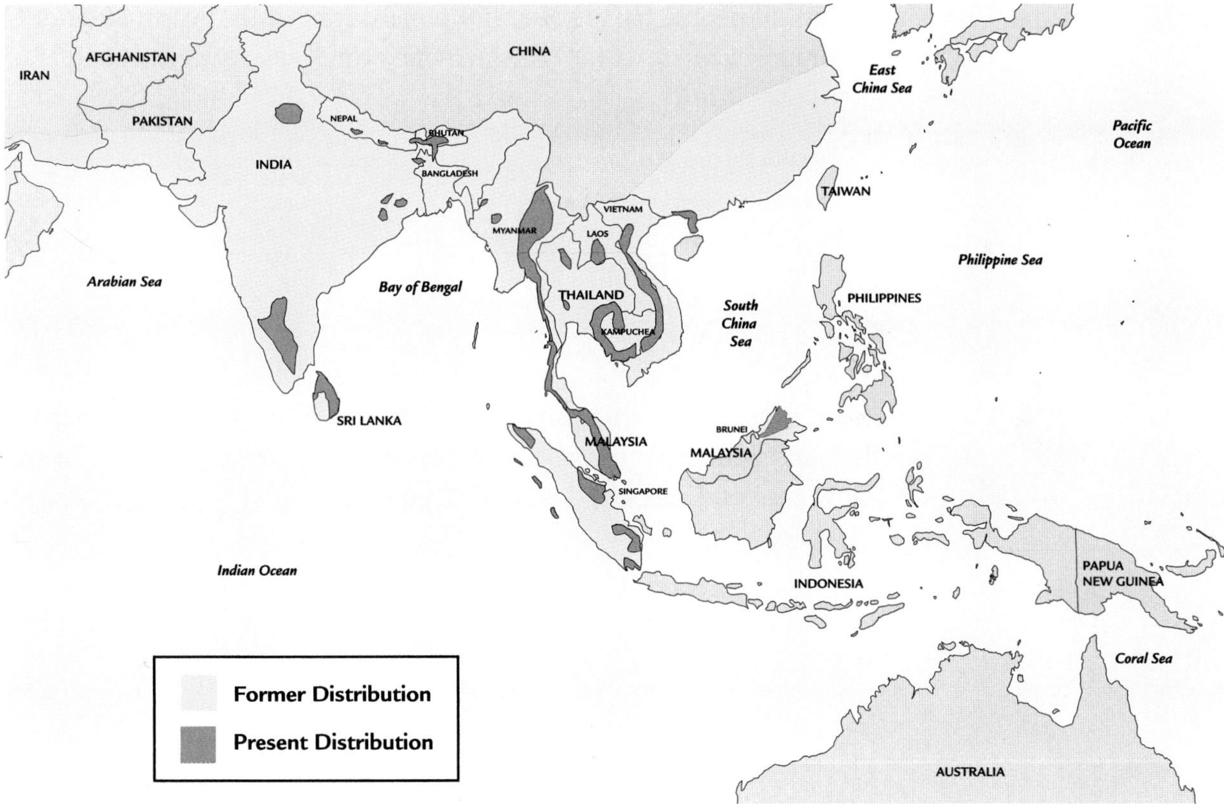

Figure 3: Historic and Current Range of Asian Elephants

ANALYSIS

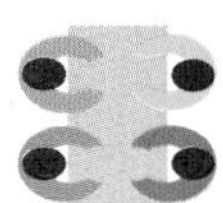

1. What are the similarities and differences between the extinction of mammoths and the possible extinction of Asian elephants?

2. Use evidence from this activity to explain why the mammoth could once have been considered an endangered species.

3. Some scientists would like to try to re-create a living mammoth by removing the DNA from a fertilized elephant egg and replacing it with mammoth DNA.

   a. Which species of elephant egg do you think scientists should try first? **Hint:** Look carefully at Figure 2.

   b. Do you think scientists should try to re-create a living mammoth? Explain.

4. Should people try to save wild populations of the Asian elephant? Support your answer with evidence and discuss the trade-offs of your decision.

   Hint: To write a complete answer, first state your opinion. Provide two or more pieces of evidence that support your opinion. Then discuss the trade-offs of your decision.

EXTENSION

Learn more about attempts to save the Asian elephant from extinction and proposals to bring the mammoth back to life. Start at the SALI page of the SEPUP website.

Figuring Out Fossils

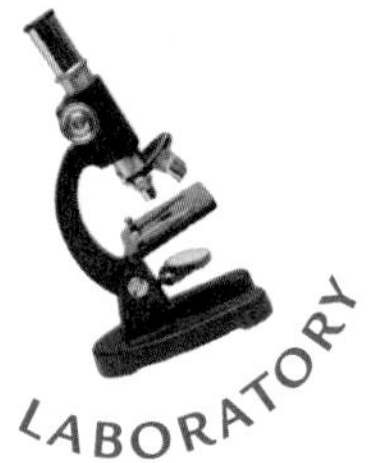

Many species have become extinct during the history of Earth. How can you know these creatures ever existed? The evidence is right under your nose—or your feet, to be more precise.

Our planet's thin outer layer, the crust, can be up to 40 kilometers (25 miles) thick. The crust is made up of many layers of rock that have been forming for over 4 billion years, and are still forming today. These rock layers can form when a volcanic eruption covers the land with lava, or when a flood spreads out a layer of mud. Lava, mud, or even sand can eventually harden into solid rock. New rock layers can also form over hundreds of years as sediment—sand, dirt, and the remains of dead organisms—gradually settles on the bottom of a lake or ocean.

Any new layer of rock can seal off the layer below it. Organisms trapped within these sealed off layers can become part of the rock itself. Any trace of life preserved in a rock is called a **fossil.** It can be an entire organism, a part of an organism, a footprint, a piece of feces, or a piece of shell, bone, or tooth.

What can fossils tell you about organisms that lived in the past?

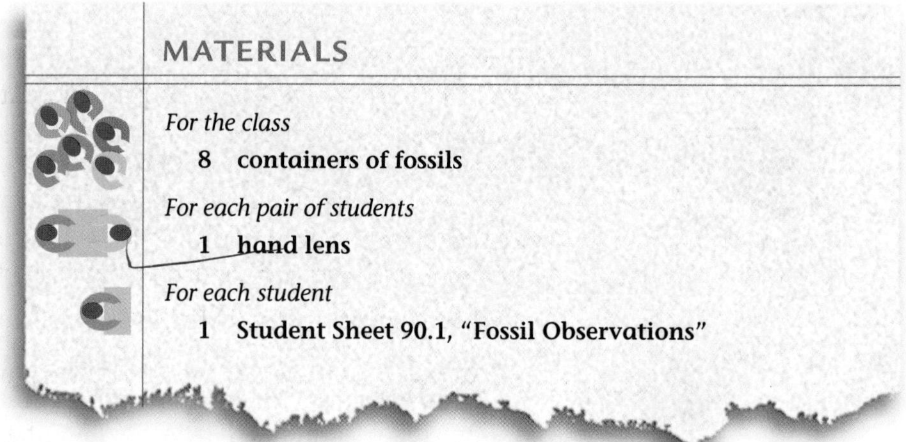

MATERIALS

For the class
8 **containers of fossils**

For each pair of students
1 **hand lens**

For each student
1 **Student Sheet 90.1, "Fossil Observations"**

PROCEDURE

1. Work in a group of four. Collect a pair of fossils. One pair in the group should begin by examining one of the fossil specimens, while the other pair begins by examining the other specimen.
2. Work with your partner to identify the unique features of the fossil. Be sure to look at both specimens of the fossil species. Use the magnifier to help you.
3. On Student Sheet 90.1, "Fossil Observations," sketch the general shape and unique features of this type of fossil. Then record additional observations that are difficult to show in your sketch, such as color or size. Note that your group of four has two specimens of the same fossil. You can write observations on both of these specimens.
4. When directed by your teacher, exchange your pair of fossils with another group of four students.
5. Repeat Steps 1 through 4 until you have examined all eight types of fossils. As you continue to look at more fossils, observe similarities and differences among the different fossils.

ANALYSIS

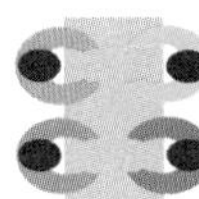

1. Review your notes on the eight different types of fossils. Do you think any of them are from similar species? Explain, using evidence from this activity to support your answer.

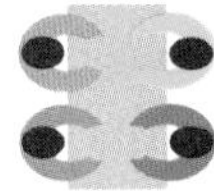

2. In this activity, you were given a fossil to examine. What additional observations could you have made about the fossil if you had discovered it yourself?

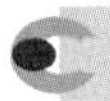

3. Choose one of the eight fossils you examined.

    a. Based on the fossil, describe what you think this organism looked like when it was alive. Include your evidence for your description.

    b. In what type of environment would you expect to find this organism? Explain your reasoning.

4. Although you probably have a vivid picture of dinosaurs in your mind, no one has ever seen a living dinosaur. All the evidence for the existence of dinosaurs comes from fossils.

    a. What details about the appearance and behavior of dinosaurs do you think would be easiest to determine from fossils?

    b. What details about the appearance and behavior of dinosaurs do you think would be hardest to determine from fossils?

91 Fossilized Footprints

Paleontologists (pay-lee-uhn-TALL-uh-jists) are scientists who study fossils. Fossils are rarely complete and are often just a shell, half a leaf, or a couple of bones. In some cases, the only evidence left by an organism is its tracks. Footprints and other types of animal tracks can be fossilized in the same way as actual body parts. But what can you find out from just footprints? Like detectives, paleontologists can use the information from fossil footprints to determine how an organism moved, how fast it traveled, what type of environment it lived in, and what it might have been doing when its footprint was formed.

Few fossil remains are as complete as this 10 million-year-old rhinoceros in Nebraska.

Fossil footprints

EVIDENCE COMES IN STEPS

A fossil footprint site has just been discovered! You take a helicopter to the location in the hope that your expertise will be useful. The rest of the team is slowly brushing away layers of sediment to carefully uncover the footprints.

Your task is to use your observations to draw inferences and then develop a hypothesis about what happened to form the footprints. As the footprints are uncovered, there will be more evidence to examine. Remain open to new possibilities as the investigation continues.

CHALLENGE

How can fossil footprints be used to study the behavior of animals that were alive millions of years ago?

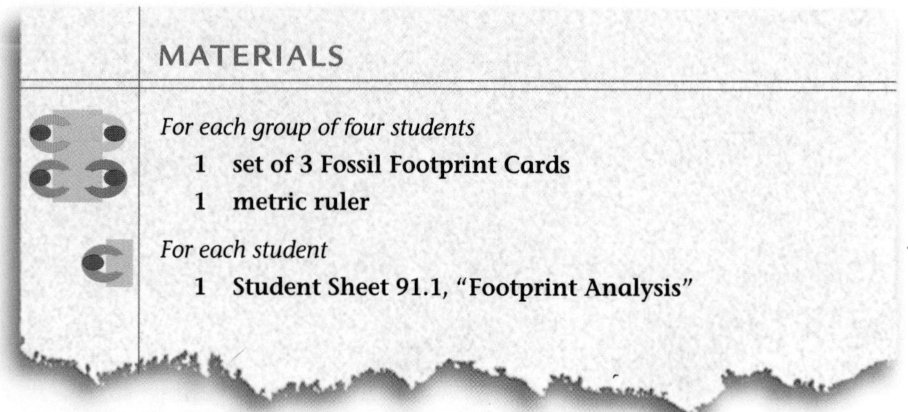

MATERIALS

For each group of four students

1 **set of 3 Fossil Footprint Cards**

1 **metric ruler**

For each student

1 **Student Sheet 91.1, "Footprint Analysis"**

PROCEDURE

1. Examine Fossil Footprint Card 1, which shows what the team has uncovered so far.
2. In your group, discuss what you think was happening while these footprints were being created. You do not have to agree, but:
   - If you disagree with others in your group about what happened, explain to the rest of the group why you disagree.
   - Listen to and consider other people's explanations and ideas.
3. Record your ideas in the first row of Student Sheet 91.1, "Footprint Analysis." Separate your ideas into observations and inferences. **Note:** Even though some of your inferences may conflict with other inferences, consider as many ideas as possible.
4. Time passes and more footprints are uncovered. Obtain Fossil Footprint Card 2.
5. Repeat Step 2. Then record your additional observations and inferences in the second row of Student Sheet 91.1. However, do not change what you wrote in the first row!
6. Time passes and a third section of footprints is uncovered. Obtain Fossil Footprint Card 3.
7. Repeat Step 2. Then record your additional observations and inferences in the third row of Student Sheet 91.1. Remember, do not change what you wrote in the first two rows!

8. Look back at all your observations and inferences. Try to think of the best possible explanation for how the footprints were formed. Record your strongest hypothesis in your science notebook. If you have two or more hypotheses in mind, record them all, but rank them from most likely to least likely.

ANALYSIS

1. Why is it important for scientists—and people in general—to distinguish between observations and inferences when they develop a hypothesis?

2. Imagine that the team uncovered a fourth section of footprints. Draw what you predict this fourth section might look like. Explain how it would provide more support for the hypothesis you favor.

3. Different types of information can be collected from footprints. In addition to observing the shape, size, and arrangements of footprints, their depths can be measured. The tables below show two different sets of measurements that might have been taken.

Table 1 Average Depths of Footprints (Scenario 1)

	Card 1	Card 2	Card 3
Larger footprints	6.0 cm	6.2 cm	8.3 cm
Smaller footprints	2.5 cm	2.6 cm	——

Table 2 Average Depths of Footprints (Scenario 2)

	Card 1	Card 2	Card 3
Larger footprints	6.0 cm	6.2 cm	6.1 cm
Smaller footprints	2.5 cm	2.6 cm	——

a. What hypotheses would the data in Table 1 support? Explain how these data would provide more evidence in support of one or more hypotheses.

b. What hypotheses would the data in Table 2 support? Explain how these data would provide more evidence in support of one or more hypotheses.

c. What factor(s) might explain the difference in the depth of the footprints in the different sections?

➢

4. **a.** Think back to an activity in which you came up with hypotheses based upon evidence, such as Activity 74, "Observing Organisms," in the Ecology unit. Describe an example of an observation and an inference based upon that observation and explain how the two are different.

   b. Describe an example of an observation and an inference from a recent event in your everyday life.

92 Time For Change

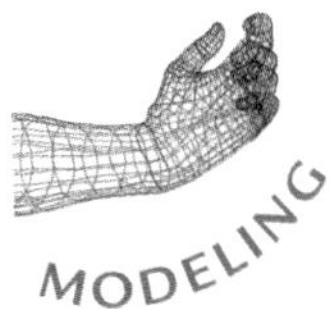

As you learned in Activity 90, "Figuring Out Fossils," the history of Earth is divided into time spans. These time spans do not last any specific number of years. The beginnings and endings of the time spans are determined by fossils—either the appearance of new types of fossils that are not found in any older rocks or the disappearance of fossils that are commonly found in older rocks. With the help of radioactive dating technology, scientists have made good estimates of how many years each time span lasted.

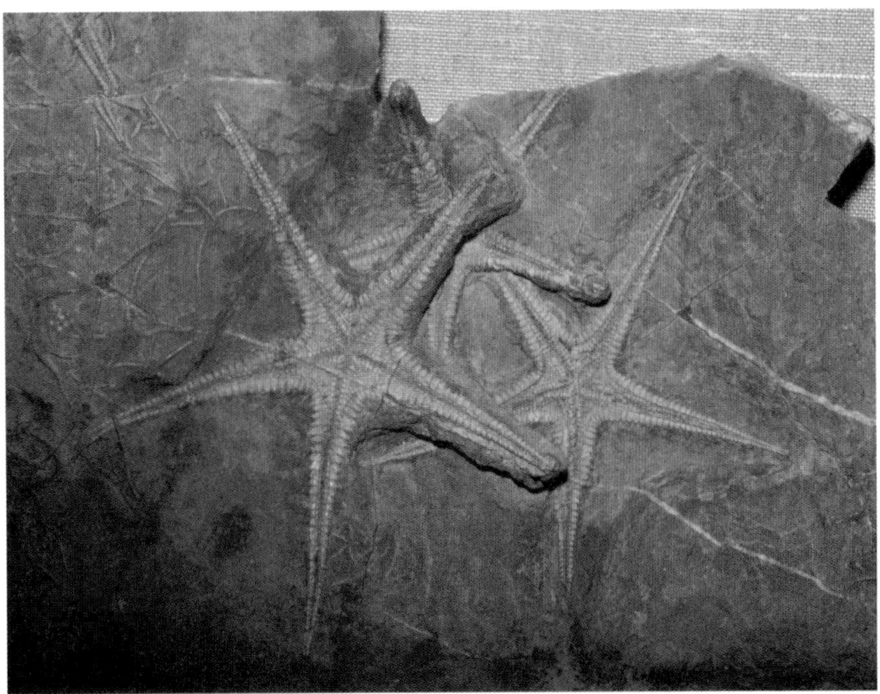

Jurassic sea star fossils

How long have organisms been living on Earth?

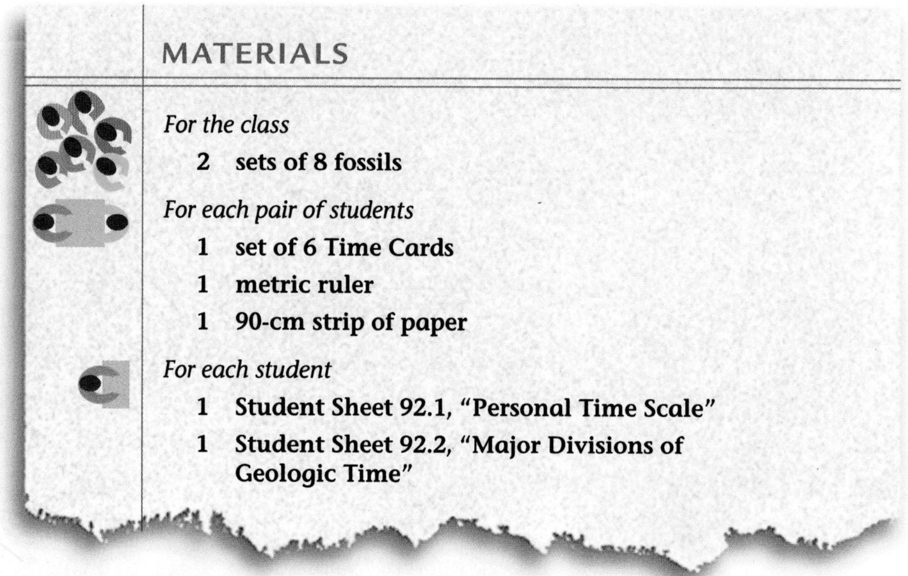

PROCEDURE

Part One: A Personal Time Scale, Geologic-Style

1. Look at the following list of events. Write the event that occurred most recently at the top of the column labeled "Order of Events" on Student Sheet 92.1, "Personal Time Scale."

   I started fourth grade.

   I ate or drank something.

   I learned to walk.

   I woke up.

   I was born.

   I took a breath.

   I started kindergarten.

   I learned to read.

   My parents were born.

2. Use the remaining spaces in the "Order of Events" column to write down the other events from most recent (at the top) to most distant (at the bottom).

3. In the column "Number of Years Ago," write the number of years ago that each event occurred (you can round off to the nearest year, or half-year). Like a paleontologist, count time backward from the present day. For example, if the event occurred 10 years ago, write "10 ya" as the time of the event. (The unit "ya" means "years ago.")

These students were born about 14 ya.

4. Think of a major event in your life that is important to you. (It may or may not already be described in your "Order of Events" column). Use this event to divide your time scale into two time periods by drawing a horizontal line to mark when the event occurred. For example, if you choose entering school as the major event, you could draw a line right below "I started kindergarten."

5. Name the two time periods that you just created. For example, if you drew a line at the time you first started school, the time period before that could be called "Pre-Schoolian."

6. As a class, compare the events that you and your classmates chose to divide your personal time scales into two periods. Work together to agree on a single event that was important to everyone in class. Agree on names for the time periods before and after that event.

➢

Part Two: Geologic Time

7. Imagine that a paleontologist asks you to help her put in order some periods of time in the history of life. With your partner, read carefully the information on the six Time Cards and arrange them with the oldest on the left and the most recent on the right.
8. In your science notebook, record the order in which you placed the cards.

Mount Rainier formed approximately one million ya (1 mya).

9. View the work of other student groups. Observe the similarities and differences between their orderings and yours. Discuss why you made the choices that you did.

10. Obtain Student Sheet 92.2, "Major Divisions of Geologic Time," and a 90-cm strip of paper from your teacher. Use the information on Student Sheet 92.2 to arrange the cards in the order scientists have determined from geologic evidence. In your science notebook, record any changes that you needed to make to your original order.

11. Follow Steps 11a–d to construct a timeline of the last 4,500 million years:

    a. Using Student Sheet 92.2, work with your partner to calculate the distance (in cm) that each time span will cover on your timeline.

       Hint: Since your timeline must represent 4,500 million years over 90 centimeters, first divide 4,500 by 90 to determine how much time each centimeter will represent.

    b. Draw a vertical line near one end of your long strip of paper and label it "The Origin of Earth."

    c. Using "The Origin of Earth" as a starting line, use a ruler and your calculations from Student Sheet 92.2 to mark the boundaries between the time spans.

    d. Label each time span with its name and each boundary with its defining event.

12. Figure 1 on the next page presents photos of the fossils you examined and sketched in Activity 90, "Figuring Out Fossils." In the appropriate time period on your timeline, draw and label a quick sketch or outline of each one.

➢

Figure 1: A Few Familiar Fossils

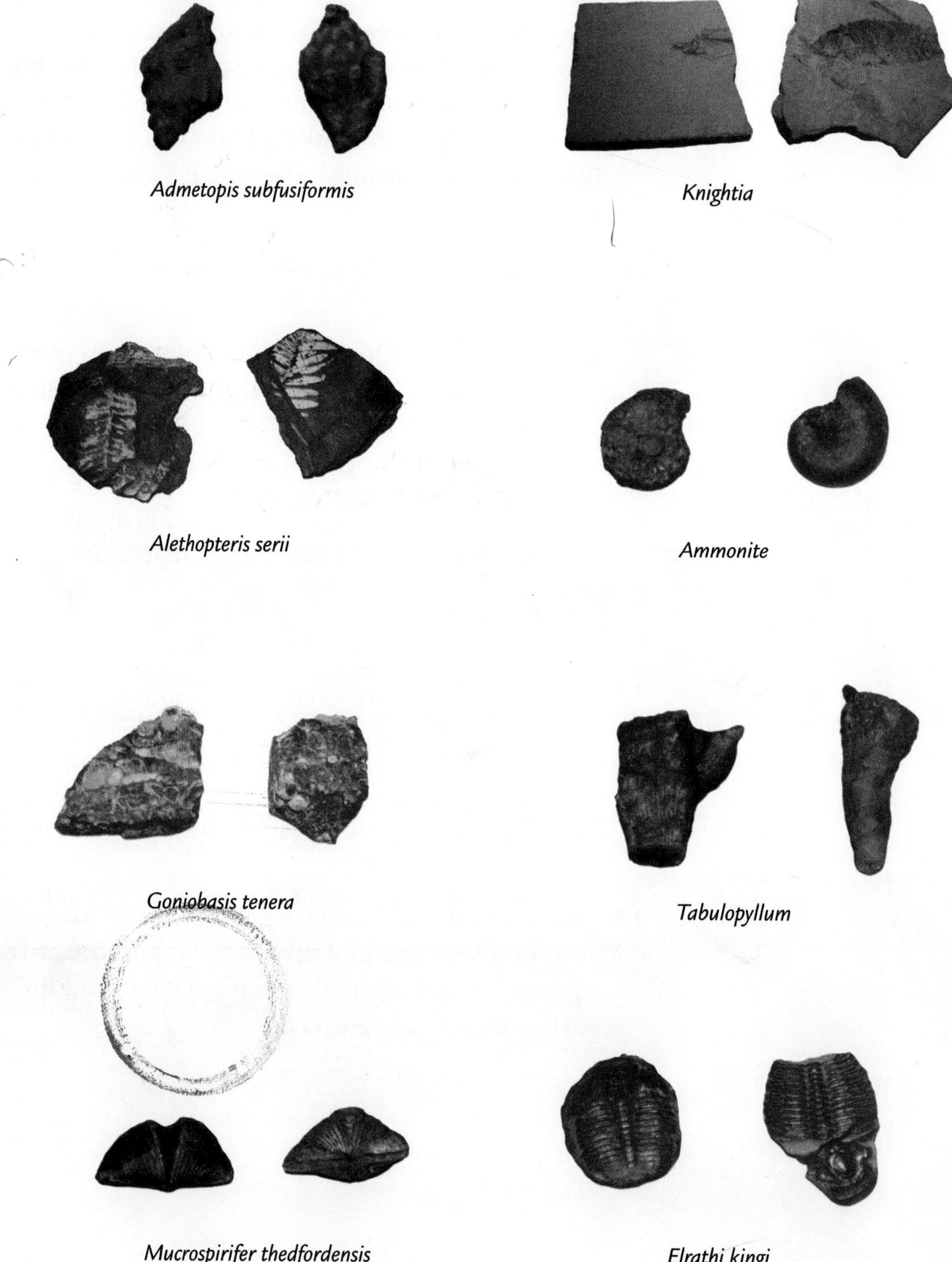

EXTENSION 1

Obtain a copy of a more detailed geologic time scale. Construct a timeline that represents only the last 550 million years. Label all the *periods* with their names and be sure to distinguish them from the *eras.* What additional information were you able to include on this timeline? What are the advantages and disadvantages of creating timelines for shorter time periods?

EXTENSION 2

As a class, create a giant timeline that represents some of the major events (such as the first fossils of interesting life forms, mass extinctions, etc.) that have occurred during the 4.5 billion-year history of Earth. Stand at appropriately scaled distances from your classmates, and together hold up signs representing major events in the history of life.

ANALYSIS

1. Think back to how you and your classmates divided your personal time scales into periods. How do you think scientists determined how to divide geologic time into its periods?

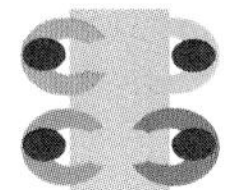

2. The total length of your timeline of Earth's history is 90 cm. Use your timeline to determine the fraction of Earth's history that:

   a. single-celled organisms have lived on our planet.

   b. multicellular organisms have lived on our planet.

3. **Reflection:** Imagine that no species ever became extinct. Do you think there would be more, less, or the same amount of diversity of life forms on our planet? Explain your answer.

93 Reading the Rocks

In some places, such as the walls of a deep river canyon, hundreds of rock layers are visible, one on top of the other. As rock layers form, each new layer is deposited on top of an already existing layer. When you observe a sequence of rock layers, the top layer, along with any fossils it contains, is younger than any other layer in that sequence, and the bottom layer, along with any fossils it contains, is the oldest layer in that sequence. This is called the **law of superposition.**

Rock layers in the Grand Canyon

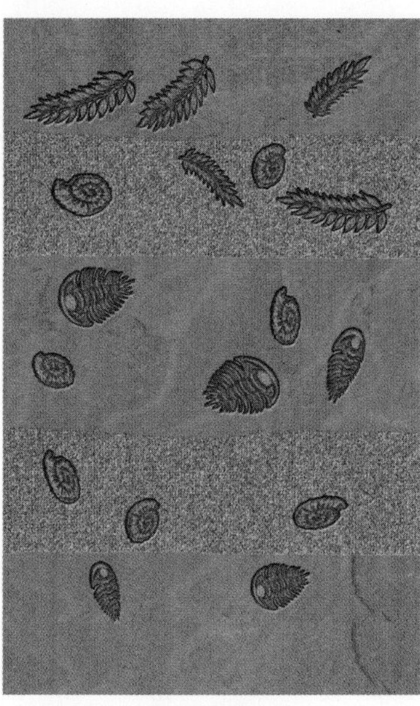

Schematic diagram of fossils in rock layers

A diagram representing a series of rock layers, such as the one on the right, is called a **stratigraphic column.** Stratigraphic columns can be made by looking at the sides of cliffs, or by looking at drill cores. A drill core is a cylindrical piece of rock removed from the Earth by a large drill, similar to the drills that are used to make oil wells. Drill cores can provide samples from many miles beneath the surface of the Earth.

No single location contains a complete set of all the rock layers or fossils that exist on Earth. In order to study a particular fossil organism or find out which organisms lived during which geologic era, paleontologists must compare rocks from different places throughout the world. You will examine and compare four different drill cores, each representing the rock layers found on different fictitious continents.

CHALLENGE

How can you determine which fossils are older, which are younger, and which are likely to be from extinct species?

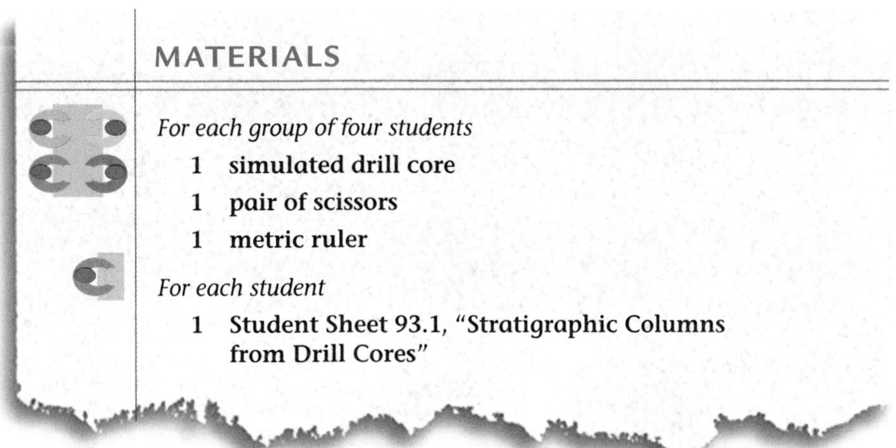

MATERIALS

For each group of four students

1 **simulated drill core**

1 **pair of scissors**

1 **metric ruler**

For each student

1 **Student Sheet 93.1, "Stratigraphic Columns from Drill Cores"**

PROCEDURE

1. Examine your drill core. The top of each drill core is marked with its number.
2. Create a stratigraphic column by sketching in the boundaries of the layers and the fossils found within each layer in the appropriate place on Student Sheet 93.1, "Stratigraphic Columns from Drill Cores."
3. Based on the evidence within the layers of this drill core, list the fossils in order from youngest to oldest.
4. When directed by your teacher, exchange your drill core with a group that has a drill core with a different number.
5. Repeat Steps 1–4 until you have observed, sketched, and analyzed all four drill cores.

6. Based on the appearance of the rock layers and the fossils found within each layer, match, or correlate, the layers from each core as best you can. Make a chart, similar to the one in Figure 1, that shows your correlation of the rock layers from the four different drill cores.

   Hint 1: You may want to cut out each column from the Student Sheet so that you can move them around as you try to match up the layers.

   Hint 2: Layers don't have to be exactly the same to correlate.

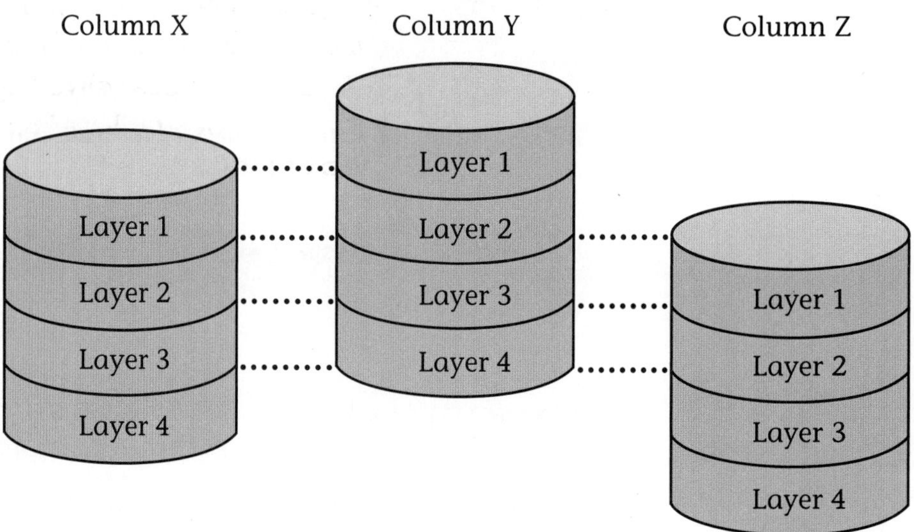

Figure 1: Sample Correlation of Stratigraphic Columns

7. Use your correlation chart to list all four of the fossils in order from youngest to oldest.

   Hint: If you think a layer found in one drill core is the same as a layer found in another drill core, you can infer that those layers, and the fossils in them, are the same age.

ANALYSIS

1. Describe some of the difficulties you had trying to match evidence found in one drill core with evidence found in other drill cores. What additional evidence would have helped you make your correlations?

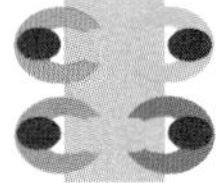

2. Based on evidence from all four drill cores, which, if any, of the organisms represented by the fossils may be from species now extinct? Explain.

3. Which fossil species could have lived at the same time?

4. Using the information below and the list you made in Step 7 of the Procedure, make a timeline that shows the time span when each species is believed to have been alive. Explain how you determined your answer and whether it is based on inference, observation, or a combination of both.

Core	Layer	Geologic Era
4	1	Early Cenozoic
1	2	Early Mesozoic
3	5	Middle Paleozoic
2	5	Early Paleozoic

Hint: Refer to Figure 1 in Activity 89, "Mammoth Mysteries," on page F-6 for help in designing your timeline.

5. **Reflection:** Propose what might have caused the changes through time shown on your timeline. Explain.

94 A Meeting of Minds

Plenty of fossil evidence shows that most of the species that have lived in the past are no longer alive today. It also seems that most of the species on Earth today were not always here. In other words, different species of organisms have lived at different times in Earth's history. New species have descended from earlier species, but have changed over long periods of time. These changes through time are called **evolution.**

But how does evolution happen? Two major theories were proposed during the 19th century. The first was disproved and abandoned, while the second has helped evolution become a central idea in modern biology. What would it sound like if the original experts met and discussed the problem?

How does evolution happen?

PROCEDURE

1. Assign a role for each person in your group. Assuming there are four people in your group, each of you will read one role.

   Roles

   Charles Darwin, 19th century scientist

   Isabel Matos, science reporter for Station W-EVO

   Jean-Baptiste Lamarck, 19th century scientist

   Wendy Chin, middle school student

2. Read the role play on the next pages aloud. As you read, think about what each character is saying.

HOW DO SPECIES EVOLVE?

Isabel Matos: In today's episode of "Time Travel News," we have brought together two of the first scientists to publish ideas on how evolution occurs. Visiting us from the 19th century are Jean-Baptiste Lamarck and Charles Darwin. Monsieur Lamarck, let's start with you.

Jean-Baptiste Lamarck: I was one of the first to recognize that species evolve. In 1809, I proposed the first theory of how evolution occurs. Allow me to explain my theory. Let's begin by talking about giraffes. Wendy, why do you think giraffes have such long necks?

Wendy Chin: To reach leaves at the tops of trees, I guess. They have to be able to get food.

Lamarck: Quite right. I began to wonder how giraffes' necks became so long.

Wendy: I bet they evolved that way.

Lamarck: But how did this evolution occur?

This is what I wanted to understand. My theory was that giraffes stretched their necks by reaching for leaves that were higher and higher on the trees. This made their necks longer. Then, when they had babies, their babies had longer necks too. Look—this sketch helps explain my ideas.

This is an adult giraffe. *The giraffe reaches for leaves slightly out of reach.* *The use of the neck causes it to lengthen slightly.* *The offspring of the giraffe also has a longer neck.*

Figure 1: Lamarckian Evolution

Wendy: Shouldn't a theory be based on evidence?

Matos: Mr. Lamarck, did you ever see an adult giraffe grow its neck longer?

Lamarck: Of course not. My idea was that the growth was very small, too small to measure in one generation.

Charles Darwin: I'd like to explain another theory, called natural selection. Alfred Russel Wallace and I constructed this theory at about the same time. We also noticed that not all animals of the same type have the same features. Take horses, for instance.

Wendy: Oh, I know what you mean! There are horses of different sizes and colors, but they are all one species and can interbreed.

Darwin: Exactly—and the same is true of giraffes. Have you noticed that animals in the same species look different, or varied? This is important because, in the wild, some animals in each species usually die every year. Only animals that survive can give birth to offspring. Now, what feature of a giraffe might help it to survive and live to reproduce?

What differences do you observe in these giraffes of the same species?

Lamarck: Its neck, of course! As I said before, it must stretch from being used so vigorously. Giraffes can then pass on the longer necks to their children.

Matos: But Mr. Lamarck, modern scientists have found no evidence for your hypothesis that parents can pass *acquired* traits to their offspring. Consider professional wrestlers. They build muscles by lifting weights. But their babies are no stronger than other babies. If these babies want to have muscles like their parents, they have to pump a lot of iron too!

Darwin: But just like human babies, not all giraffes are the same. They have slight differences in all their characteristics, including neck length.

Lamarck: So you're saying any giraffe that happens to have a slightly longer neck can eat leaves that are higher in a tree than a shorter-necked giraffe can and therefore is more likely to survive.

➢

Wendy: So the longer-necked giraffes are more likely to live longer because they can reach more food. If more of these giraffes live longer, they can produce more offspring!

Darwin: That's right. Animals with certain features, such as giraffes with longer necks, are more likely to live to adulthood and have more babies. We call that process **natural selection**. Here's a sketch of how it works

Giraffes with longer necks tend to reach leaves more easily.

Longer-necked giraffes are more likely to eat enough to survive . . .

. . . and reproduce. The offspring inherit their parent's longer necks.

Figure 2: Darwinian Evolution (Natural Selection)

Wendy: But why will the offspring of longer-necked giraffes have longer necks too?

Matos: Well, tall parents are more likely to have tall children, aren't they? The same is probably true of giraffes.

Darwin: According to my theory, each new generation of giraffes has, on the average, slightly longer necks than the generation before.

Lamarck: But not because they stretched their necks? Only because the longer-necked giraffes were more likely to survive and reproduce?

Wendy: I get it. Individual animals don't change, but over very long periods of time, the population of an entire species does.

Lamarck: But, Mr. Darwin, can your theory of natural selection explain why extinction occurs?

Darwin: I believe so. Consider the mammoth, which became extinct a few thousand years ago. Why didn't mammoths evolve and continue to survive?

Wendy: There are several theories about that. They became extinct during a time when the global climate was warmer than it had been before. The changing climate may have affected the mammoth's food supply, and human hunters may have contributed to the extinction.

Matos: So a species becomes extinct when it doesn't survive an environmental change. No individuals in the population have the traits necessary to survive.

Darwin: That's all it is. The **variation** in the population isn't enough to withstand environmental changes. In fact, sooner or later, most species become extinct.

Wendy: Let me get this straight. As time passes, species change, and we call this evolution. The way this occurs is by natural selection—some individuals in a population happen to be better suited to the environment and they're more likely to survive and reproduce.

Lamarck: As a result, the population as a whole over many generations comes to have an **adaptation**, such as a giraffe's longer neck.

Matos: Today, we know that we pass on characteristics like longer necks to our offspring through genes. Genes don't change because you exercise your neck.

Darwin: Tell us more about these genes.

Wendy: I learned about genes in school. Genes are things in our cells that we inherit from our parents. They cause us to have traits—the way we look and stuff.

Lamarck: Fascinating. I would like to learn more about this.

Darwin: Without this modern evidence, I hesitated to publish my theory for years, until Wallace sent me a brief paper containing the same ideas. Within a few years of our publications, scientists widely accepted the idea that species arise by descent with modification, or evolution.

Matos: Thank you, Mr. Lamarck and Mr. Darwin. Viewers, I hope you've enjoyed meeting people from our past. Join us next week for a scintillating conversation with Marie Curie, the first woman scientist to receive a Nobel Prize.

ANALYSIS

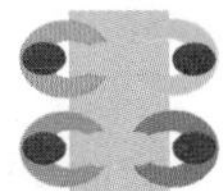

1. **a.** Compare and contrast Lamarck's and Darwin's theories of evolution: What are the similarities? What are the differences?

   b. Why do scientists find Darwin's theory more convincing?

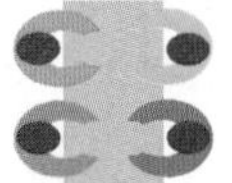

2. Ancestors of modern elephants had much shorter trunks than elephants do today. Use Lamarck's theory of evolution to explain how the trunks of elephants might get longer over many generations. Drawing a picture may help you to explain what you have learned.

3. Use the Darwin/Wallace theory of natural selection to explain how the trunks of elephants might get longer over many generations. Drawing a picture may help you to explain what you have learned.

4. **Reflection:** If you have completed Unit C, "Micro-Life," of *Science and Life Issues,* look back at Activity 51, "The Full Course," and Activity 52, "Miracle Drugs—Or Not?" to review antibiotic-resistant bacteria. How is the problem of antibiotic resistance in bacteria an example of natural selection?

95 Hiding in the Background

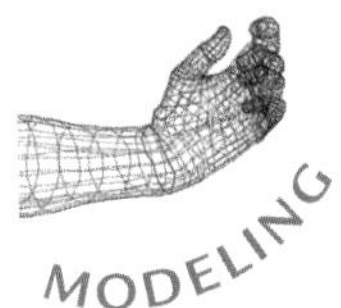

In the last activity, you considered the interaction between the environment and a species over a long span of time. You saw that the location of leaves on trees could affect which giraffes survived. Over many generations, longer-necked giraffes would be more likely to reach the uppermost leaves on tall trees. This might make them more likely to survive, reproduce, and pass their traits on to their offspring. If this were to happen, longer necks would be called an adaptation to the tall-tree environment.

Adaptations that make a species more successful are not always traits that make the species stronger, bigger, or faster. For example, some adaptations decrease the chances that a species will be eaten by another species. Adaptations of this type include the skin colors of lizards, the spines of porcupines, and the scent glands of skunks.

CHALLENGE

How do factors such as the environment and the presence of predators affect the process of natural selection?

THE TOOTHPICK WORM MODEL

Imagine that you are a bird that eats small worms. In this activity, toothpicks of two different colors will represent the worms that you eat.

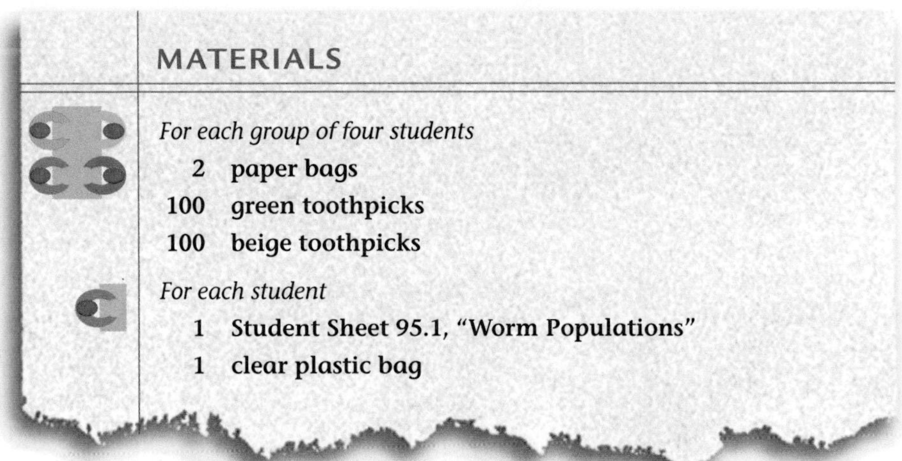

MATERIALS

For each group of four students

2 **paper bags**
100 **green toothpicks**
100 **beige toothpicks**

For each student

1 **Student Sheet 95.1, "Worm Populations"**
1 **clear plastic bag**

PROCEDURE

1. Label one of the paper bags "Worms" and the other "Reserve Toothpicks."
2. Each toothpick represents a worm. Count 25 green "worms" and 25 beige "worms" and place them into the paper bag labeled "Worms." This is the initial number of worms. These amounts are already marked for you in both tables on Student Sheet 95.1, "Worm Populations" (Table 1 is for green worms and Table 2 is for beige worms).
3. Place the rest of the toothpicks into the bag labeled "Reserve Toothpicks."
4. Shake the "Worms" bag to mix the worms.

5. As directed by your teacher, scatter the worms on the "ground."

6. You are going to play the role of a bird that eats worms. Each person in your group "eats" (picks up) the first 10 worms he or she sees and places them into the clear plastic bag, which represents the bird's stomach.

7. Count the total numbers of green and beige worms eaten by your group. Record these totals in Row 2 of each table on Student Sheet 95.1. Be sure to stay in the column for this generation.

8. *Some worms are still alive.* Subtract the number of worms that your group "ate" from the initial population in that generation. For example, if your group collected 18 green worms, there must be 7 green worms still alive on the ground (25 – 18 = 7). Record the numbers of surviving green and beige worms in Row 3 of each table on Student Sheet 95.1.

9. *Each living worm is reproducing.* On Student Sheet 95.1, multiply the numbers of green and beige worms still alive by 4. For example, if you had 7 green worms still alive, there would be a total of 28 green offspring worms (7 x 4 – 28). Record this number in Row 4.

10. Add one toothpick for each new green and beige worm into your paper bag labeled "Worms." For example, if your group had 7 green worms surviving on the ground, you would add 28 green toothpicks to the paper bag.

11. On Student Sheet 95.1, add Rows 3 and 4 of each table to calculate the final populations of green and beige worms. Record these numbers in Row 5 of each table. Record these same numbers in Row 1 in the columns for the *next* generation.

12. Repeat Steps 4–11 for Generation 2. If you have time, perform the simulation for further generations.

EXTENSION

Repeat the activity wearing a pair of sunglasses with green lenses. How are your results different?

➢

ANALYSIS

1. **a.** Determine the ratio of green to beige worms in each generation. For example, the ratio of green to beige worms in Generation 1 is 25:25, or 1:1.

   b. Describe how the ratio of green to beige worms changed over the three generations.

   c. Why do you think this change occurred? Explain.

2. Imagine that you performed this simulation for another generation. What do you predict the ratio of green to beige worms would be? Explain your prediction.

3. Due to a drought, grass begins to dry out and die, leaving only dead grass stalks. What is likely to happen to the ratio of green to beige worms? Explain.

4. **a.** In this activity, what effect did the environment have on the process of natural selection?

   b. In this activity, what role did the predator (bird) have in the process of natural selection?

5. **Reflection:** Why do you think earthworms are beige and not green?

96 Battling Beaks

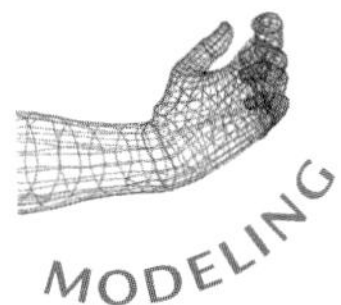

During the history of Earth, species have both evolved and become extinct. Why do some species survive to reproduce while others do not?

What role does variation play in the process of natural selection?

Why do these four different species of birds have such different beaks?

THE FORKBIRD MODEL

In this activity, you will role-play a single species called "forkbirds." Forkbirds feed by either spearing or scooping their food. During feeding time, each bird gathers "wild loops" and immediately deposits them in its "stomach" before gathering more food. Your goal is to gather enough food to survive and reproduce. This will allow you to pass your genes on to another generation. Occasionally, a forkbird offspring will have a genetic mutation that makes it look different from its parent.

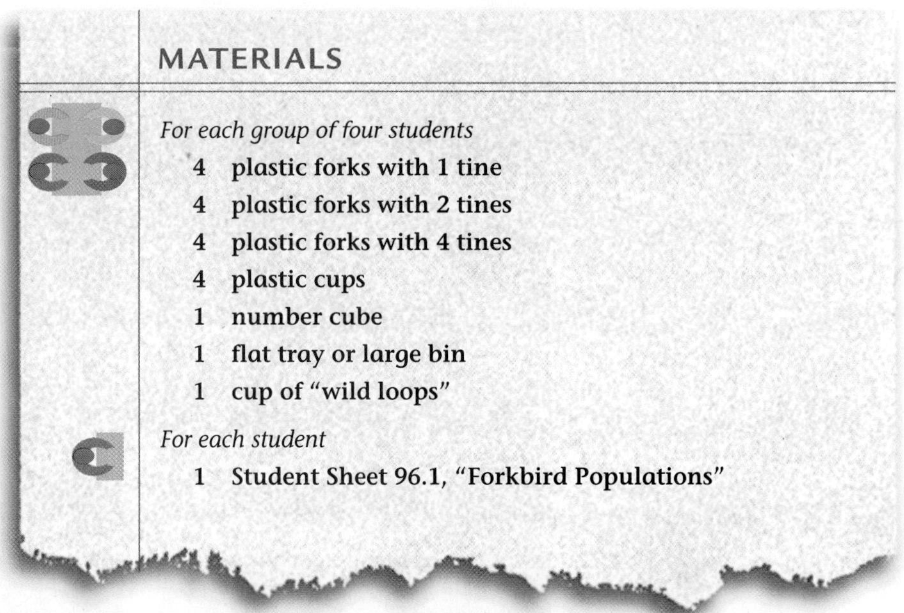

MATERIALS

For each group of four students

4 plastic forks with 1 tine
4 plastic forks with 2 tines
4 plastic forks with 4 tines
4 plastic cups
1 number cube
1 flat tray or large bin
1 cup of "wild loops"

For each student

1 Student Sheet 96.1, "Forkbird Populations"

PROCEDURE

1. The initial forkbird population has beaks with only two tines. Each person in your group should begin the activity with a 2-tined fork. Record the initial population of each type of forkbird in Table 1 of Student Sheet 96.1, "Forkbird Populations."

2. Your teacher will tell you when feeding time begins, and then all of the forkbirds can feed.

3. When feeding time ends, count the number of wild loops eaten by each forkbird. Within your group, the two forkbirds that gathered the most food survive to reproduce. (If there is a tie for second place, then three forkbirds survive. The two forkbirds that tie should keep their forks and skip Step 4.)

4. The two surviving forkbirds should each toss the number cube. Use the table below to determine the type of beak of the offspring of each surviving forkbird. The group members whose forkbirds did not survive should now assume the roles of the offspring.

Number Cube Key

Your Toss	Forkbird Offspring
1	1-tined forkbird
2	2-tined forkbird
4	4-tined forkbird
3, 5, 6	same as parent forkbird

5. Record the new population of each type of forkbird in your group in the next row on Student Sheet 96.1.

6. Return all of the wild loops to the "forest floor" (tray or bin) to simulate the growth of wild loops.

7. Repeat Steps 2–6 for nine more rounds to represent additional generations.

8. Share your data with the class. As a class, record the population of each type of forkbird over many generations. Be sure to copy the class data onto Student Sheet 96.1.

9. Create a graph of the class totals of each type of forkbird over many generations. You can plot the data for all three types of forkbirds on a single graph. Be sure to title your graph, label your axes, and provide a key.

➢

ANALYSIS

1. Which type of forkbird was the most successful? Explain how the class data support this conclusion.

2. **a.** Look at your graph of the class results. Describe what happened to the number of each type of forkbird over many generations.

   b. In the forkbird model, mutations at reproduction were much more common than they are in real life. Imagine that the number of mutations was lowered, so that the vast majority of offspring had beaks similar to those of their parents. Predict what you think would have happened to the numbers of each type of forkbird in future generations.

3. How did the forkbird activity simulate the process of natural selection? Explain.

4. The forkbirds that you studied are a single species. Although they look slightly different, they are part of a single, interbreeding population. Imagine that a change in the food supply occurred.

   a. As a result of heavy rains, the major source of forkbird food is now soft berries, like blueberries. After many, many generations, how many types of forkbirds do you think will be in the population? Explain your reasoning.

   b. As a result of a drought, the major source of forkbird food is now sunflower seeds. After many, many generations, how many types of forkbirds do you think will be in the population? Explain your reasoning.

5. **Reflection:** The cheetah, an extremely fast and efficient hunter, is an endangered species. The few cheetahs alive today show very little variation. How does this help to explain why cheetahs are on the verge of becoming extinct?

97 Origins of Species

In Activity 92, "Time For Change," you saw that the types of living organisms have changed throughout Earth's history. Where do all of the new types of organisms come from?

What role do mutations play in natural selection?

Three different species of bears

READING

In the Ecology unit, you learned that each species has a particular role within its ecosystem. The angelfish is adapted to eating small aquatic worms. To people, most adult angelfish of a particular breed appear the same: they are all of similar size and coloration and eat the same types of food. But there is some variation—every angelfish is slightly different (Figure 1). Consider other organisms that you might think are identical. What could you do to identify differences among individuals within the species?

Figure 1: Variation Between Two Angelfish

One way to look for variation is to examine physical features, such as color and shape. Often, features like the width or pattern of stripes on an angelfish are slightly different from one fish to the next. Since some physical differences are due to genetic differences, they can be passed along through the generations.

STOPPING TO THINK 1

Think about similarities and differences among ten different people you know.

a. What are some physical features that are likely to be a result of genetic differences?

b. What are some physical features that may not be a result of genetics, but a result of some other factor(s), such as development from birth to adulthood?

c. What are some physical features that might be a result of both genetics and other factors?

In Activity 96, "Battling Beaks," you modeled a forkbird population that showed variation. Although all the forkbirds were from the same species, there were 1-tined, 2-tined, and 4-tined forkbirds. What was the source of these differences?

All genetic variation exists because of **mutations**. The reproduction of the genetic material does not always happen perfectly. As a result, occasionally an offspring has features that do not exist in the parents or even in the rest of the species. Most mutations are harmful. For example, a bird might be born with a beak of such unusual shape that the bird cannot feed. Such mutations are not passed on to the next generation, since the affected organism does not survive to reproduce.

In other cases, a mutation is neither helpful nor harmful. The 1-tined forkbird from the previous activity was an example of this type of mutation. Even though it was not as successful as the 4-tined mutation, the 1-tined beak was neither helpful nor harmful when compared to the 2-tined beak. Since there was no advantage or disadvantage to this type of beak, the 1-tined forkbird did not die out in the population.

STOPPING TO THINK 2

Imagine that you own a dog that recently gave birth to a litter of puppies. Your veterinarian informs you that one of the puppies has a genetic mutation.

a. Think of a mutation that the puppy could have that would be neither helpful nor harmful.

b. Think of a mutation that the puppy could have that would be harmful.

In some cases, a mutation is helpful. Imagine that a bird from a species that eats small nuts is born with a larger beak than the rest of the population. The larger beak allows this bird to eat large nuts as well as smaller nuts. If nuts became harder to find, this mutation could help this bird survive and reproduce. Any larger-beaked offspring might continue to be more successful than the rest of the bird population. After many generations, all of these birds might have larger beaks (Figure 2). In the previous activity, the 4-tined forkbird was an example of a helpful mutation.

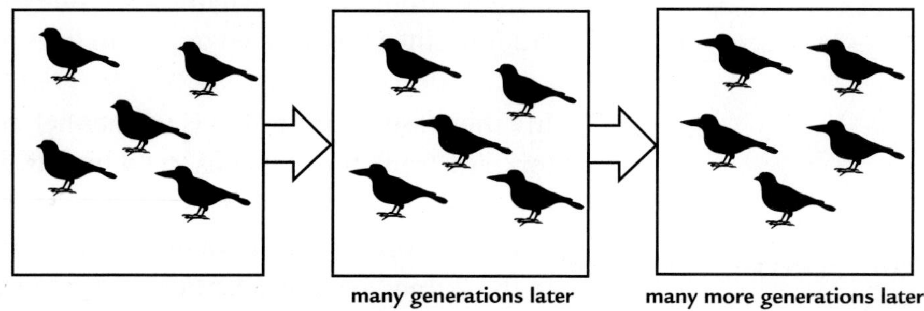

Figure 2: Evolution of Larger-Beaked Birds
As a result of a helpful mutation occurring just once, an entire population of birds might look very different after many generations.

In a new environment, natural selection might favor a mutation that is not favorable in the original environment. If this population eventually can no longer successfully reproduce with the population it came from, it is considered a different species.

STOPPING TO THINK 3

You may have heard someone who is wrapping a present say, "I wish I had another hand!" Explain why an organism cannot choose to have a mutation that would enable it to live more successfully in its environment. For example, could birds choose to have larger beaks? Explain your reasoning.

Figure 3: The Galapagos Islands

The fossil record provides evidence that many different species have lived during the history of Earth. But Charles Darwin was one of the first people to notice that living species also provide evidence for evolution. In the late 1830s, Darwin traveled on a ship called the *Beagle* that sailed around the world. He collected evidence and made careful observations of the natural world wherever the voyage took him. One of the places that the ship stopped was the Galapagos Islands, a chain of islands located in the Pacific Ocean, west of South America (Figure 3).

In the Galapagos Islands, Darwin collected samples of many different species, including 14 species of finch (a small bird). All of the finches were similar, but the species varied in color, size, and beak shape. Darwin observed a relationship between the shape of a finch's beak and the food that it ate. Scientists had noticed that the beak of each species was particularly well-adapted to getting a specific type of food, such as a certain seed or insect (Figure 4).

Cactus finch

Large ground finch

Warbler finch

Figure 4: A Few Galapagos Finches

Based on his observations, Darwin hypothesized that all 14 different finch species had evolved from one single ancestral species. He proposed that, thousands or even millions of years ago, a single species of South American finch migrated and began nesting on the islands. Over many generations, different adaptations proved more successful on one island than on another. Because each island is separated by some distance from others in the chain, the finch population on each island is relatively small and isolated. This allowed helpful genetic mutations to spread within a population—by natural selection—more quickly than usual. Eventually, changes in beak shapes, combined with the spread of other helpful mutations, resulted in enough differences that the various finches became separate species, each adapted for a different ecosystem role.

Today, scientists use genetic evidence to compare similarities and differences among species. By testing the genes of the various finches, scientists have shown that the finches are very closely related, providing more evidence that Darwin's hypothesis is correct.

STOPPING TO THINK 4

Darwin identified 14 species of finch on the Galapagos Islands. Your friend says that this means only 14 mutations occurred within the finch populations. Explain whether you agree with your friend and why.

But you don't need isolated islands to produce new species. Remember the Nile perch of Lake Victoria in Africa, which you studied in the previous unit? One consequence of the introduction of these large fish into the lake was the extinction of up to 200 species of just one type of fish—the cichlid.

Different species of cichlids

How did so many species of the same fish family ever come to exist in a single lake? A single lake provides a surprising number of different places to live and ways to survive. Differences in the amount of light, wind, mud, sand, temperature, plants, predators, and insects produce a variety of habitats within one lake. Lake Victoria provides so many different habitats that over 300 different species of cichlids had evolved within the lake before the introduction of the Nile perch.

Are all of these cichlids really descended from a single ancestor? Every line of evidence suggests this is so. Modern genetic evidence indicates that all the cichlids in Lake Victoria evolved from a common ancestor within the last 200,000 years. That's a short period of time in terms of evolution!

ANALYSIS

1. Are mutations always helpful? Explain.

2. How can mutations enable the evolution of a new species to occur? Use the story of the cichlids to help you explain your ideas.

3. Under ideal conditions, bacteria have a generation time of about 20 minutes. Humans have a generation time of about 20 years. Which would you expect to evolve faster? Why?

98 Family Histories

Fossils have been found in Precambrian rocks 3.5 billion years old. But most have been found in rocks of the Paleozoic, Mesozoic, and Cenozoic eras, which are all less than 550 million years old. The types of organisms found in different rocks can provide important information about the history of life on Earth. The term **fossil record** refers to all of the fossils that have been found on Earth.

The fossil record has been used to classify fossils into families. A family is a category smaller than a kingdom, phylum, class, or order, but larger than a genus or species. For example, dogs are in the family Canidae, which also contains foxes, jackals, coyotes, and wolves. Lions are in the same kingdom, phylum, class, and order as dogs, but they are in a different family: Felidäe. This family includes leopards, tigers, cheetahs, house cats, and extinct species such as the saber-toothed cat. You will investigate how the numbers of families in the fish, mammal, and reptile classes have changed over geological time.

What can you learn about evolution by comparing the fossil records of fish, mammals, and reptiles?

Classifying Carnivores

Classification Level	Dogs	Lions
Kingdom	Animalia	Animalia
Phylum	Chordata	Chordata
Class	Mammalia	Mammalia
Order	Carnivora	Carnivora
Family	**Canidae**	**Felidae**
Genus	*Canis*	*Panthera*
Species	*familiaris*	*leo*

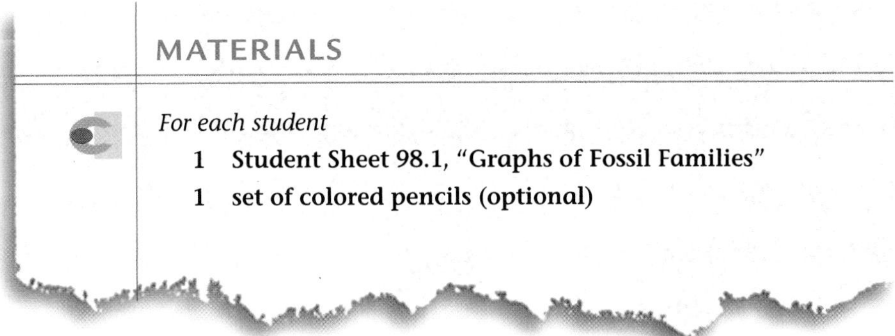

MATERIALS

For each student

1 **Student Sheet 98.1, "Graphs of Fossil Families"**

1 **set of colored pencils (optional)**

PROCEDURE

1. Table 1 below provides the history of all the families of fish currently known from the fossil record. When a fossil is found that does not belong to any family found in *earlier* geologic time periods, we call it a "first appearance." It is the first appearance of that family in the fossil record. When a fossil is found that does not belong to any family found in *later* geologic time periods, we call it a "last appearance." It is the last appearance of that family in the fossil record. Look at Table 1 and discuss the following questions with your partner:

- Between which years did the greatest number of fish families appear in the fossil record? In what era was this period of time?
- Between which years did the greatest number of fish families disappear from the fossil record? In what era was this period of time?

Table 1: History of Fossil Fish Families

Era	Precambrian	Early Paleozoic			Late Paleozoic		Mesozoic			Cenozoic
Time (mya)	>545	485	425	365	305	245	185	125	65	0
Number of first appearances	0	25	43	162	67	13	52	33	84	299
Number of last appearances	0	9	31	158	49	48	36	20	44	34

➢

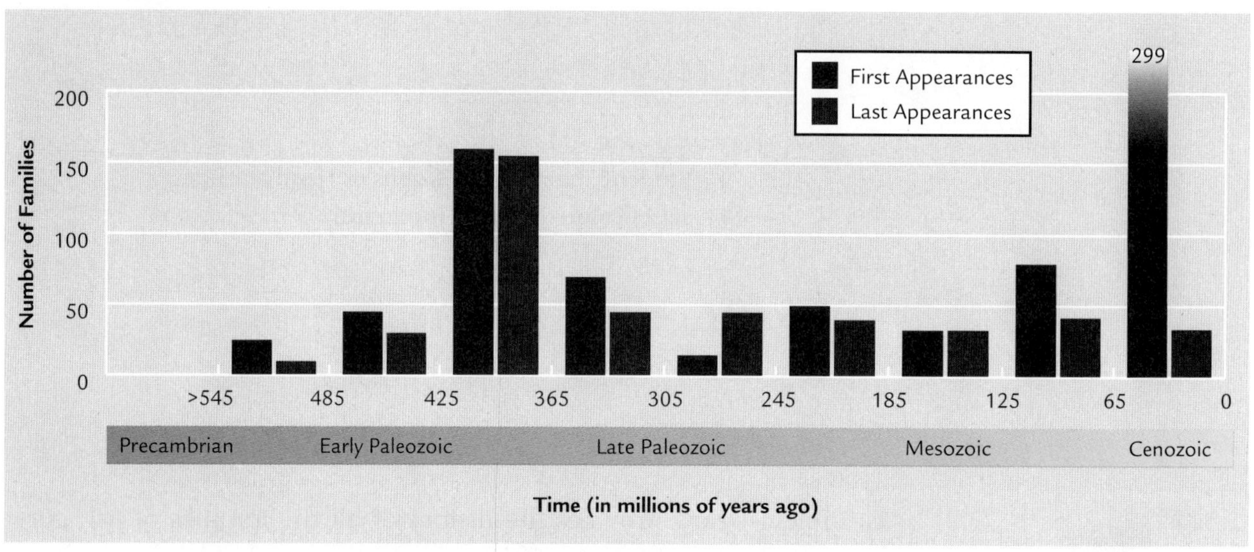

Figure 1: Graph of Fossil Fish Families Over Time

2. Figure 1 presents a double bar graph of the data shown in Table 1. Look at the graph and discuss with your partner in what ways the graph makes the data easier to interpret.

3. Use the information in Table 2 to make a double bar graph for families of reptiles, similar to the one for fish shown in Figure 1. Since you will be comparing graphs, be sure to use the same scale on the y-axis.

Table 2: History of Fossil Reptile Families

Era	Precambrian	Early Paleozoic			Late Paleozoic		Mesozoic			Cenozoic
Time (mya)	>545	485	425	365	305	245	185	125	65	0
Number of first appearances	0	0	0	0	3	67	95	68	97	35
Number of last appearances	0	0	0	0	1	57	93	46	84	26

Table 3: History of Fossil Mammal Families

Era	Precambrian	Early Paleozoic			Late Paleozoic		Mesozoic			Cenozoic
Time (mya)	>545	485	425	365	305	245	185	125	65	0
Number of first appearances	0	0	0	0	0	0	6	14	33	404
Number of last appearances	0	0	0	0	0	0	2	8	33	262

4. Use the information in Table 3 to make a double bar graph for families of mammals, similar to the one for fish shown in Figure 1. Since you will be comparing graphs, be sure to use the same scale on the y-axis.

A familiar example of a fossilized reptile

ANALYSIS

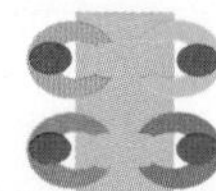

1. **a.** Use the graphs to place the three different classes in order, based on when they first appeared in the fossil record.

   b. What could this order tell you about the evolution of these types of species?

2. **a.** What are some possible explanations for the disappearance of a family from the fossil record?

   b. How could Darwin's theory of natural selection explain the disappearance of these families?

3. What could explain the appearance of a family in the fossil record?

4. **a.** The Cenozoic Era is often referred to as the "Age of Mammals." Using evidence from this activity, explain why.

   b. Based on evidence from this activity, what could you call the Mesozoic Era? Explain your reasoning.

   c. Look at the appearances and disappearances of families over time on all three graphs. Why is it misleading to label an era as the "age of" any particular class?

99 A Whale of a Tale

Whales, dolphins, and porpoises are mammals that live in the sea. Like all mammals, they are warm-blooded animals that give birth to live young and need air to breathe. DNA evidence shows that whales are closely related to hoofed land mammals such as hippopotamuses, pigs, cows, and sheep. All of these mammals are thought to have descended from a single species that lived millions of years ago and is now extinct. Besides DNA evidence, what other evidence suggests that these animals are related?

How are modern and fossil skeletons used to investigate evolution?

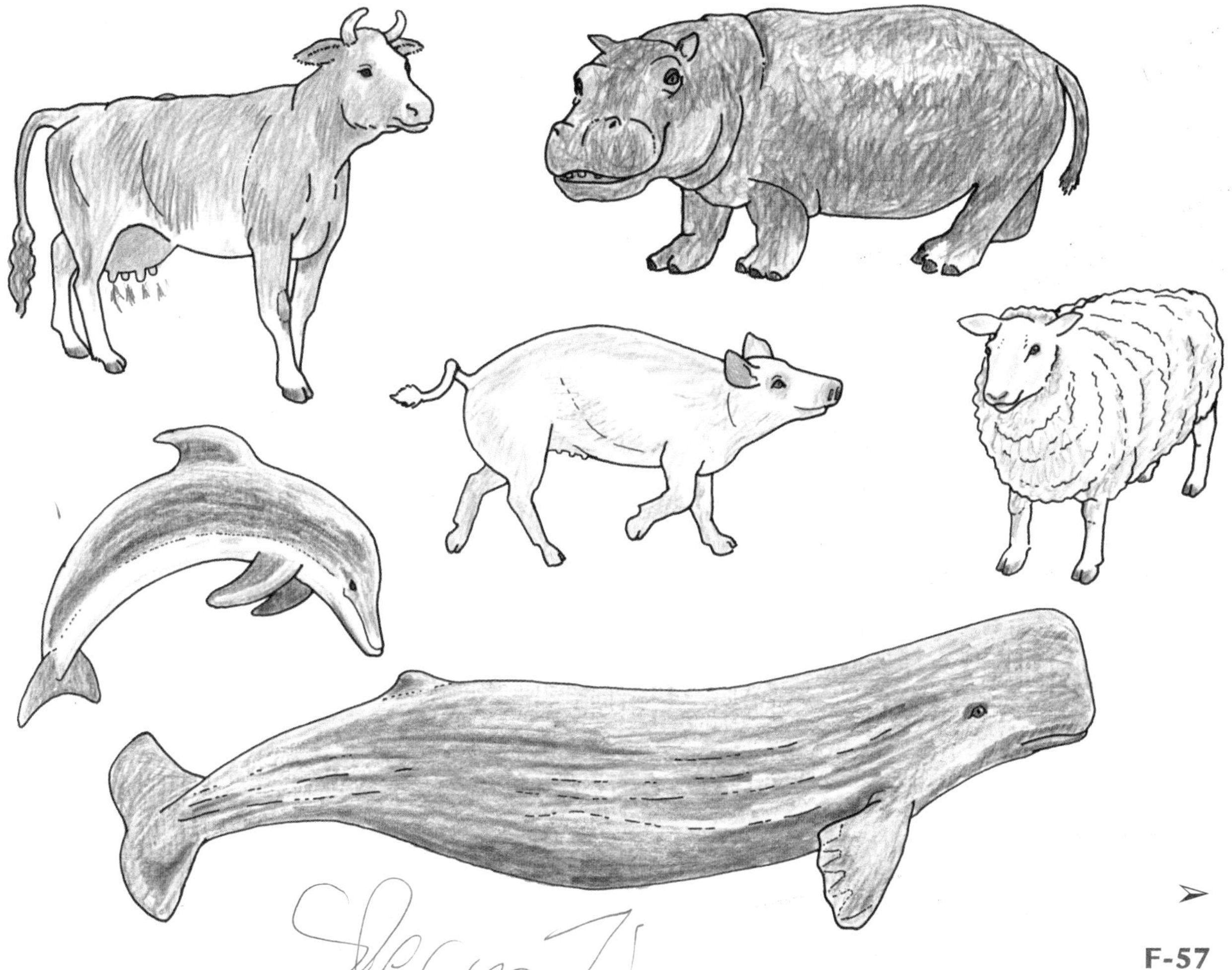

THE FOSSIL EXHIBIT

You've just been hired as the assistant curator of the fossil collection of a museum. On your first day, you discover that the skeletons in the exhibit on the evolution of whales have all been moved to a new room and need to be arranged. Unfortunately, you are not a whale expert and the skeletons are not clearly labeled.

A local middle school has scheduled a field trip to the museum. It is very important that you arrange the skeletons properly before the students arrive. You decide to examine them to see if you can figure out how they should be arranged.

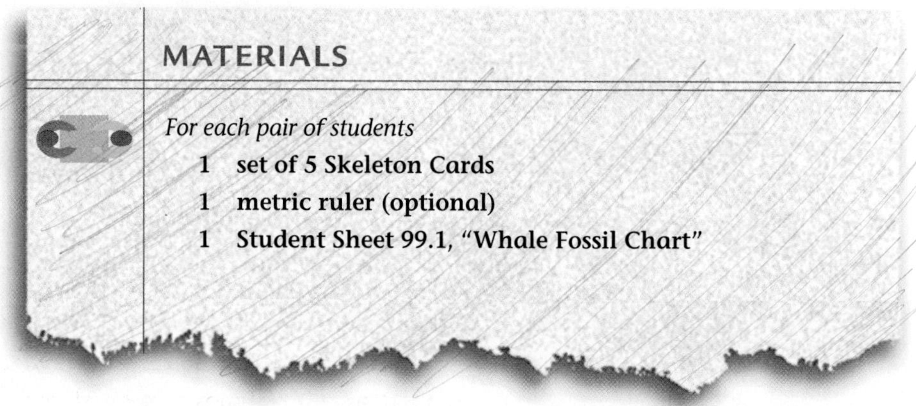

MATERIALS

For each pair of students

1 **set of 5 Skeleton Cards**
1 **metric ruler (optional)**
1 **Student Sheet 99.1, "Whale Fossil Chart"**

PROCEDURE

1. Compare the five Skeleton Cards. Based on similarities you observe, group the skeletons into two sets, each containing two or three cards. The set of skeletons containing Skeleton A should be called "Group 1." The other set of skeletons will be "Group 2."

Comparing Skeletons

	Similarities	Differences
Group 1 skeletons: A, ________		
Group 2 skeletons: __________		
Group 1 skeletons compared with Group 2 skeletons		

2. Create a table in your science notebook like the one shown above. In the first column, record which skeletons you put in each group.

3. Compare the skeletons *within* each group. In your table, describe and record as many similarities and differences as you can.

4. Compare Group 1 skeletons with those of Group 2. In your table, describe and record as many similarities and differences as you can.

5. *It's time to figure out how to arrange the exhibit!* Use similarities and differences in the skeletons to arrange the cards in order. (While all five skeletons can be in a single line, they don't have to be.) Record the order in which you have arranged the skeletons. **Hint:** Place the two least similar skeletons on either side of your desk. Then arrange the other three skeletons between them.

6. *You're in luck! You discover a chart with information about the relative ages of the five skeletons.* Collect Student Sheet 99.1, "Whale Fossil Chart," from your teacher.

7. Compare the age data from Student Sheet 99.1 with the order in which you placed the skeletons in Step 5. If necessary, rearrange your Skeleton Cards. Record your final reconstruction of the museum exhibit in your science notebook.

➢

ANALYSIS

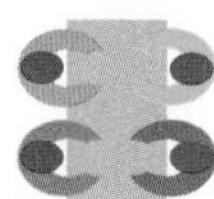

1. **a.** What kinds of skeletal changes appear to have occurred during the evolution of whales?

   b. What can you infer about the changes in habitat that occurred at the same time as these skeletal changes?

2. Use natural selection to explain how these changes (or one of these changes) could have occurred.

3. In this activity, you examined extinct and modern whale skeletons. How does the study of these skeletons provide evidence about how species are related?

4. Look again at Skeleton A. This is known as an ambulocetid (am-byoo-low-SEE-tid). The word *ambulocetid* means "walking whale." Where do you think the ambulocetids lived? Describe how you think they lived.

EXTENSION

Find out more about current research on whale evolution. Start at the SALI page of the SEPUP website.

Numbers of Differences Between DNA Sequences

	Mammal #1	Mammal #2	Mammal #3	Reptile
Fish				
Mammal #1	—			
Mammal #2	—	—		
Mammal #3	—	—	—	

3. In Activity 99, "A Whale of a Tale," you examined evidence that whales are mammals. Look again at your DNA samples. Discuss with your group whether these samples provide additional evidence that whales are mammals.

Part Two: Gathering More Evidence

4. In Activity 76, "People, Birds, and Bats," you classified a number of vertebrates into different classes. Review how you classified four of these animals: the kiwi, platypus, armadillo, and bat.

5. A local biotechnology center provides you and the geneticist with DNA samples from these four animals. Use Student Sheet 100.2, "Unusual Vertebrates," to compare the DNA samples of these four animals with the DNA samples from Part One. In your science notebook, create a table similar to the one above to record your comparisons.

6. In your science notebook, record whether the DNA evidence supports or conflicts with the way that you had classified these animals. If you make any changes to your classification, be sure to record them.

➢

ANALYSIS

1. In this activity, you used DNA to evaluate relationships among animals. How does DNA provide evidence about how species are related?

2. Would you expect the DNA of a seahorse to be more like the DNA of a horse or the DNA of a trout? Use evidence from this activity to support your answer.

3. **a.** Look back at the evolutionary tree in Figure 2 of Activity 89, "Here Today, Gone Tomorrow?" Draw a simple tree that shows the evolution of reptiles, fish, and mammals.

   b. Explain how DNA evidence helps you draw evolutionary trees.

4. The first mammals evolved from a reptilian ancestor, 200 million years ago. Explain why it is not accurate to say that humans evolved from lizards.

EXTENSION

Compare the human, chimpanzee, and rhesus monkey DNA sequences provided on Student Sheet 100.3, "Comparing Primates." Use this evidence to draw an evolutionary tree for these three types of primates.

101 Birds of a Feather?

By comparing fossil evidence with living species, it is clear that almost all the species that have ever lived on Earth have become extinct. As this diagram shows, most living species are descended from a small fraction of the species that have ever existed.

Wherever a "branch" of this evolutionary tree of species ends, an extinction occurred (except at the present day).

Why do some species survive while others disappear? Species die out for many reasons. These include environmental change, competing species, habitat loss, and disease. Human activity can contribute to each of these causes.

How does natural selection help explain the extinction of the dodo bird and the success of the common pigeon?

➢

PROCEDURE

Compare the fate of the dodo bird with that of the common pigeon.

RELATED BIRDS, DIFFERENT FATES

The common pigeon seems to be everywhere—almost everyone has seen one of these birds. No one alive today has seen a dodo bird, and no preserved specimens of this extinct species exist. There are 27 orders of birds. Based on skeletal comparisons, the dodo and the pigeon are classified in the same order. The pigeon and the dodo are evolutionary cousins!

The Dodo Bird

Often portrayed as flightless, fat, slow, and stupid, the dodo bird (*Raphus cucullatus*) has become a symbol for something out-of-date or clumsy. Some people think it somehow fitting that the dodo species went extinct. How could natural selection have produced such a creature in the first place?

Dodos lived successfully for several million years on the island of Mauritius in the Indian Ocean (Figure 1). Migratory birds probably had settled on Mauritius long before, just as Darwin's finches did on the Galapagos Islands. Contrary to popular belief, evidence shows that the flightless dodo was a slender, fast-running animal (Figure 2). Although it competed for resources with many other bird species, the 30- to 50-pound dodo had few predators on the island. Without predators, dodos could nest on the forest floor and eat fruit that fell from trees. Flight was unnecessary for survival and so, over many generations, the new species evolved to become flightless.

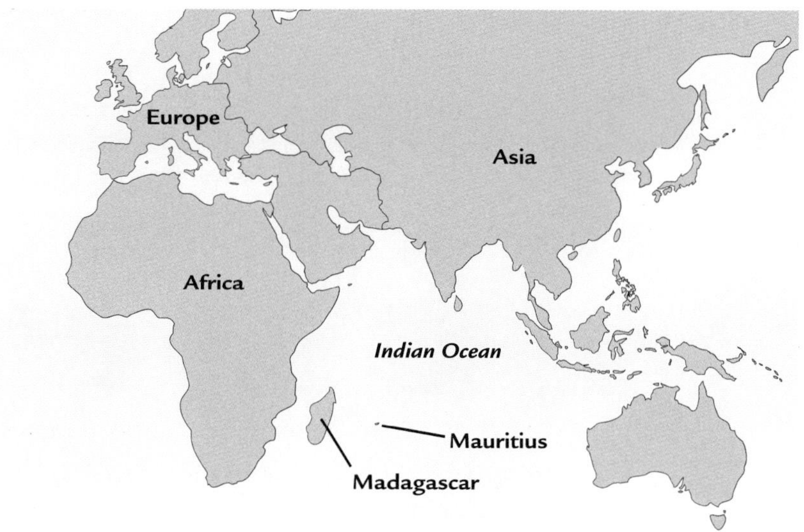

Figure 1: Location of Mauritius
Mauritius is a volcanic island about 10 million years old, about 500 miles east of Madagascar. Today, it is an independent country with a population of over 1 million people.

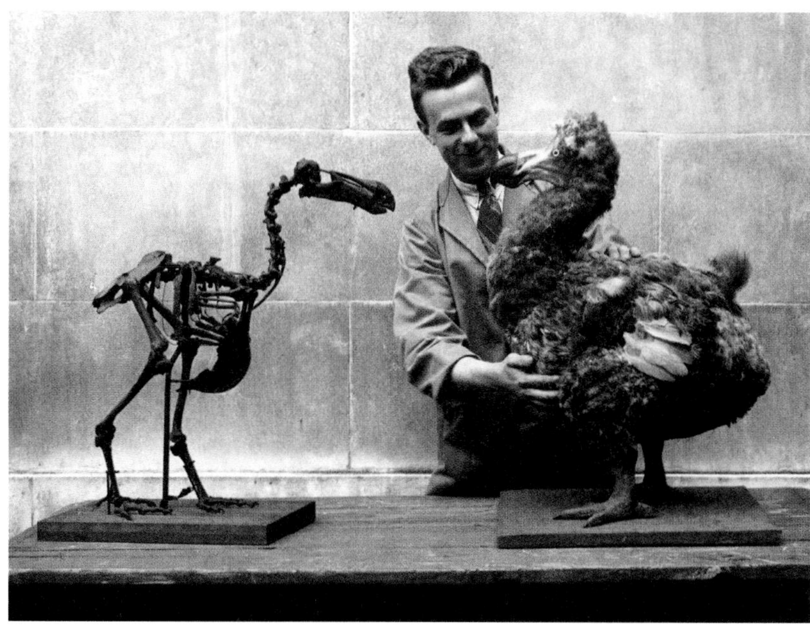

Figure 2: What Remains of the Dodo
Made of bones gathered from the island during the 1850s, this skeleton confirms that the dodo was flightless, but not that it was slow-moving.

Penguins, as well as the kiwi (shown on page E-25), are examples of living species of flightless birds.

In 1505, Portuguese sailors became the first mammals to set foot on Mauritius. Soon, the island became a common stopping place for ships travelling between Europe and Asia. Because of its large size and inability to fly, the dodo became a hunting target for hungry sailors. Because dodo nests were on the ground, their eggs were easily found and eaten by the rats, pigs, monkeys, and other animals that accompanied the sailors. In addition, human settlers' need for cleared land and wood greatly reduced the size of the dodo's forest habitat. In 1681, less than 200 years after the first predators arrived on Mauritius, the last dodo bird was killed.

The Common Pigeon

Native to Europe and Asia, pigeons now thrive on five continents. The common pigeon, or rock dove (*Columba livia*), was first domesticated by humans between five and ten thousand years ago. Early humans raised the birds for food, and pigeon meat is still a delicacy in many cultures. Later, pigeons were bred to race, to deliver messages, to do stunts, and for show (Figure 3).

Perhaps even before becoming domesticated, pigeons discovered that human structures were convenient, safe places to nest. In addition, fields and marketplaces provided an easy-to-gather, year-round food supply. During their several thousand years of close association with humans, human-bred pigeons have escaped and mated with wild pigeons, sharing genes with them. As a result, pigeon populations found near people, known as feral pigeons, are quite different from wild pigeons. They can fly faster and for longer distances, breed earlier in life, produce more offspring, and live at a much higher population density. The remaining population of wild pigeons is decreasing, and may soon dwindle to zero. Meanwhile, the population of feral pigeons continues to grow.

Figure 3: Pigeon Diversity
Over many generations, through both natural processes and breeding, the pigeon species has evolved adaptations to many successful lifestyles associated with the human species.

➢

ANALYSIS

1. If humans had never interacted with either the dodo or the pigeon, how do you think the history of each species would be different? Explain your reasoning.

2. Could the evolution of feral pigeons be described as the formation of a new species? Explain.

3. Use natural selection to explain how the flying bird that first settled on Mauritius might have evolved into the flightless dodo. In your answer, be sure to include the role of mutations.

4. Your friend argues that the dodo bird became extinct because it was a poorly adapted species, destined for failure. Do you agree? Explain.

5. Imagine that advances in science and technology allow genetic engineers to re-create living dodo birds and mammoths.

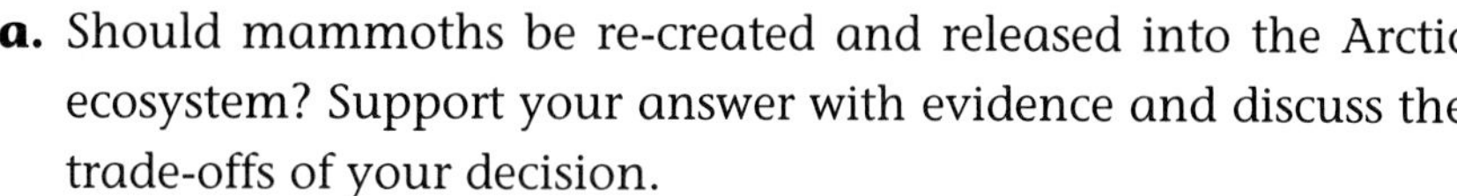

a. Should mammoths be re-created and released into the Arctic ecosystem? Support your answer with evidence and discuss the trade-offs of your decision.

b. Should dodos be re-created and released into the ecosystem of modern Mauritius? Support your answer with evidence and discuss the trade-offs of your decision.

Hint: To write a complete answer, first state your opinion. Provide two or more pieces of evidence that support your opinion. Then discuss the trade-offs of your decision.

EXTENSION

Find out more about extinct and endangered species. Start at the SALI page of the SEPUP website.

Index

A **bold** page number identifies the page on which the term is defined.

D

E

K

L

M

N

T

V

W

Y

Z

Credits

Abbreviations: t (top), m (middle), b (bottom), l (left), r (right)

All illustrations were done by Seventeenth Street Studios.

Activity icon photo, "Talking It Over": ©Michael Keller/The Stock Market

Cover photo (kids running): ©2001 David Young-Wolff/Stone

Unit E

Unit opener (E-2, E-3): tl: ©Lynda Richardson/CORBIS; tm: Sylvia Parisotto; bl: ©Dan Guravich/CORBIS; m: ©Australian Picture Library/CORBIS; mr: Sylvia Parisotto; bm: ©Anna Clopet/CORBIS; br: Dr. Herbert Thier

E-5 ©Liam Dale by permission LDTV, England; E-6 ©Frank Lane Picture Agency/CORBIS; E-10 ©S. van Mechelen, courtesy of the Exotic Species Graphics Library; E-12 t: ©Buddy Mays/CORBIS, b: courtesy of Jack Leonard, New Orleans Mosquito Control Board; E-13 t: © O. Alamany & E. Vicens/CORBIS, b: California Department of Food and Agriculture; E-14 b: Martha L. Walter, Michigan Sea Grant; E-15 ©Lynda Richardson/CORBIS; E-16 ©Joel W. Rogers/CORBIS; E-23 tl: Dr. Herbert Thier, tm: ©W. Wayne Lockwood, M.D./CORBIS, tr: ©Stephen Frink/CORBIS, bl: ©Michael & Patricia Fogden/CORBIS; E-25 t: ©Papilio/CORBIS, b: ©Buddy Mays/CORBIS; E-28: l: ©Brandon D. Cole; E-29 ©Neil Rabinowitz/CORBIS; E-32 ©Morton Beebe, S.F./CORBIS; E-33 ©Neil Rabinowitz/CORBIS; E-43 GLSGN Exotic Species Library; E-44 ©Frank Lane Picture Agency/CORBIS; E-47 map courtesy of the U.S. Geological Survey; E-52 ©AFP/CORBIS; E-59 ©Gary Braasch/CORBIS; E-67 GLSGN Exotic Species Library; E-72 ©2001 Ben Osborne/Stone; E-80 Stephen Stewart, Michigan Sea Grant; E-81 Ron Peplowski, Detroit Edison, Monroe Michigan Power Station; E-83 Steve Krynock; E-85 ©Kevin Fleming/CORBIS

Unit F

Unit opener (F-2, F-3): tl: Roberta Smith; tm: ©Charles Mauzy/CORBIS; bl: Roberta Smith; m: ©Kevin Schafer/CORBIS; mr: ©Jonathan Blair/CORBIS; bm: ©Lester V. Bergman/CORBIS; br: Donna Markey

F-4 tl:©C.Iverson/Photo Researchers, Inc., tr:©Bettmann/CORBIS, br: ©Kevin Fleming/CORBIS; F-7 tr: ©2001Manoj Shah/Stone F-14 ©Annie Griffiths Belt/CORBIS; F-15 ©Francesc Muntada/CORBIS; F-19 ©Kevin Schafer/CORBIS; F-21 ©2001 Lori Adamski Peek/Stone; F-22 ©Charles Mauzy/CORBIS; F-37 br: ©W. Perry Conway/CORBIS; F-41 bl: ©Gary W. Carter/CORBIS, br:©George Lepp/CORBIS; F-46 ©F. McConnaughey/Photo Researchers, Inc.; F-49 Images courtesy of Dr. Robert Rothman; F-50 l: ©Papilio/CORBIS, r: ©Sea World, Inc./Corbis; F-67 br: ©Hulton-Deutsch Collections/CORBIS; F-69 l: ©2001 Cesar Lucas Abreu/The Image Bank, r: Annie Griffiths Bell/CORBIS; F-70 ©David & Peter Turnley/CORBIS